Message from the author

こんにちは！or if this is the first time we are "meeting," 初^{はじ}めまして！

My name is Jeremy and thank you very much for checking out my t[...] Japanese grammar textbook I have had the pleasure of writing, and where my first book [...] the basic aspects of Japanese grammar, this book goes into a little bit more advanced material. So, if you are already familiar with most JLPT level 4 and some level 3 level structures and vocabulary, this book should be perfect for you in helping take your Japanese to the next level.

Learning another language can be a very difficult task to undertake, but at the same time, extremely rewarding. The important thing to remember is to stick to it! Learning Japanese has been one of the greatest things I have done to enrich my life. I hope, with a little bit of help from my book, it can do the same for you.

I have taken what I have learned from my own experiences as a student of the language to help explain various details in a clear and understandable way for those who were just like me when I started my language learning adventure. I hope that this book can help you in achieving your own goals, whatever they may be; work, travel, or just to make friends.

Thanks again and 頑張^{がんば}ってください！

Also, I want to thank all of my friends and family for the support they have given me over the years. And I want to give a very special thanks to 美緑 without whom I never would have finished this book, and who did a fantastic job editing and designing. 心^{こころ}よりありがとうございます！

About the Book

Pro-Tips: You will find these sections sprinkled throughout the book. They give interesting or helpful pieces of advice on various subjects.

Japanese Onomatopoeia (擬音語^{ぎおんご}): Like the Pro-Tips, you will find these sections sprinkled throughout the book. 擬音語^{ぎおんご} are "words" that consist of four syllables and are used to describe various things by how they "sound;" likes states of being or even feelings. Japanese people love to use onomatopoeia in daily conversations. So by studying them you can help make your Japanese sound much more native and improve your listening skills as well! わくわく〜!

Practice: Throughout the chapters you will find Practice Problems that will help test your understanding of the material. Check you work with the answer key in the back, but please keep in mind that your answers might not always match what is written in the key exactly. For English to Japanese translation exercises, for example, you may use a different word or expression in your answer. That is perfectly fine. There are multiple ways to express the same thing. Simply use the Answer Key as a guide in these cases.

Audio tracks now available!

I am very happy to announce that audio tracks are now available for the example sentences in this book!

A *huge* ありがとう! goes to 美緑 for all of the hard work she put in to lending me (and you, dear reader) her beautiful voice.

You can find the audio files here: LearnJapaneseFromSomeGuy.com/audio

There, you can listen online or download the different chapter tracks to your device.

As you go through the chapters, listen to and read along with the example sentences to help train your ear to pick up the Japanese sounds and to check how your pronunciation matches up with a native speaker's.

Again, I am very excited to be able to offer this to you. I hope you find them useful.

よろしくお願いいたします！

Kanji and Vocabulary words

Write down any new Kanji characters or vocabulary words that you encounter as you study this book so that you can reference them easily and study them again later.

No.	Kanji / Word	Meaning	No.	Kanji / Word	Meaning
1			21		
2			22		
3			23		
4			24		
5			25		
6			26		
7			27		
8			28		
9			29		
10			30		
11			31		
12			32		
13			33		
14			34		
15			35		
16			36		
17			37		
18			38		
19			39		
20			40		

Table of Contents 目次

Japanese Onomatopoeia

Chapter 1
Using 「こと」

In this chapter, we are going to focus on the various ways to use 「こと.」 Some of the explanations will be a review of what was touched on in my previous book (of course, a little review never killed anybody), but most of the following structures will be new to you (unless you've seen them somewhere else... in which case, they will not be new to you). Anyway, I feel that learning to harness the power of 「こと」 will, with relatively little effort, help send your Japanese abilities to Mt. Fuji-esque heights. So, let's get started!

I. Nominalization with 「こと」

Even though my word processor indicates (via a red squiggly line) that 'nominalization' is not a word, I assure you that it is. And unless you can recall your elementary school grammar lessons, you may not know exactly what it means. But don't worry! I will explain.

'Nominalization' is what I imagine George Bush would refer to as "nounification;" that is, turning something that is *not* a noun such as an adjective, adverb, or verb *into* a noun. The purpose of this may not seem apparent at first, but you will see, as you continue your studies, how pivotal a role it plays in the Japanese language.

Let's check out some example sentences pairing *verbs* with 「こと」 to help illustrate:

1. 彼の言うことは聞いたほうがいい。
   You should listen to what he says.

2. 彼女が僕の誕生日を忘れたことは全然気にしてない。
   Her forgetting my birthday doesn't bother me at all.

3. 肉を食べないことは体にいいと言われている。
   They say that not eating meat is good for you.

4. 彼女は日本語を勉強していることを誰にも言ってない。
   She hasn't told anybody about her studying of Japanese.

In the above four examples we can see that 「こと」 has been paired with a verb in its dictionary-form, a verb in its past-tense-form, a verb in its ない-form, and a verb in its ている-form. This was done to show just how flexible the use of 「こと」 can be.

If you are still uncertain about how nominalization, or 'nounification,' works or what it is, please take another look at the above examples. The underlined words are essentially acting as nouns, even though they contain verbs. You can replace the underlined portions with any noun, and the sentences will still make sense. For instance, using example sentence 1, we could replace "what he says" with "music;" giving us "You should listen to music" (I suggest The White Stripes). Or, using example sentence 3, we could replace "not eating meat" with "poison;" giving us, "They say that poison is good for you." Keep in mind that the veracity of the last statement has nothing to do with its grammatical correctness.

Now let's check out some sentences that pair *adjectives* with 「こと」.

5. 東京には<u>楽しいこと</u>がいっぱいあるよ。
   There are many fun things in Tokyo.

6. 子供のころ<u>大変なこと</u>があった。
   When I was a child, something really serious/awful happened.

7. <u>安くないこと</u>はどうでもいい。
   The fact that it is not cheap doesn't matter.

8. 彼が寿司<u>嫌いということ</u>を忘れていた。
   I had forgotten about the fact that he doesn't like sushi.

Again, we can see that we can replace a noun with the underlined words to make a grammatically correct sentence. Using example sentence 8, we could say, "I had forgotten about the <u>job interview</u>." Or, using example sentence 7, we could say, "<u>Age</u> doesn't matter."

IMPORTANT!
Please note that when coupled with a な-adjective, we *must* also append 「な」 before 「こと,」 as in example sentence 6.

The concept of nominalization may seem a bit tricky at first, but you will see *a lot* of it as you progress through your studies. And if you have read my first book, you should already be somewhat familiar with the concept, though you may not know it. For example, when we want to talk about our past experiences, we might say something like

Ex. 日本に<u>行ったこと</u>がある。
I have been to Japan before.

Here, we are pairing 「こと」 with the casual-past-tense form of the verb 「行く」 to show that 'the experience of having been to Japan' exists, which would be more naturally translated into English as "I have been to Japan before."

2

At this point, you may be wondering, "But Jeremy, is nominalization *really* that important?" And the answer to that is an emphatic YES. The reason being is that many grammatical structures can only be coupled with nouns. Knowing how to turn a verbal or adjectival phrase into a noun will prove to be extremely useful. And with practice, you will find yourself *nounifying* with little or no effort at all.

Let's try a little practice. Unscramble the following words to make complete sentences. For an extra challenge, try reading only the English sentences and come up with the Japanese sentence on your own.

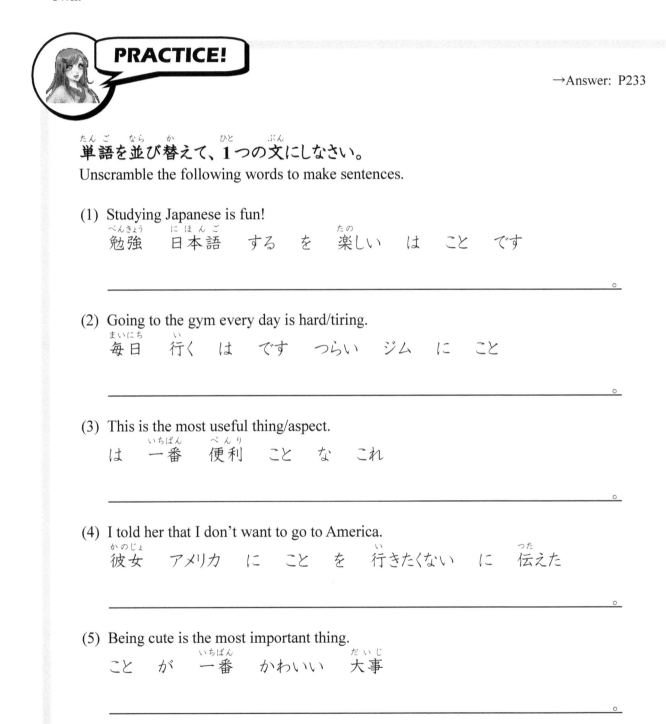

PRACTICE!

→Answer: P233

単語を並び替えて、1つの文にしなさい。
Unscramble the following words to make sentences.

(1) Studying Japanese is fun!
勉強　日本語　する　を　楽しい　は　こと　です

_____ 。

(2) Going to the gym every day is hard/tiring.
毎日　行く　は　です　つらい　ジム　に　こと

_____ 。

(3) This is the most useful thing/aspect.
は　一番　便利　こと　な　これ

_____ 。

(4) I told her that I don't want to go to America.
彼女　アメリカ　に　こと　を　行きたくない　に　伝えた

_____ 。

(5) Being cute is the most important thing.
こと　が　一番　かわいい　大事

_____ 。

3

Some Guy's Pro-Tip

It is also worth mentioning here that we aren't strictly confined to using 「こと」 when nominalizing. 「の」 may also be used for this purpose. Let's check out an example:

Ex 1. ボクシングをするのは楽しい。

Ex 2. ボクシングをすることは楽しい。

Both of these sentences could be translated as "Boxing is fun." 「の」 and 「こと」 aren't always interchangeable, however. And to keep things simple, we won't focus on using 「の」 in this way for now. Just keep in mind that you may see 「の」 being used instead of 「こと」 for this purpose.

Japanese Onomatopoeia – "Sounds of rain"

【しとしと】   Rain falling so lightly that it doesn't make a sound.
Ex. 家の外に出たら、雨がしとしとと降っていた。
     When I went outside, I saw it had been drizzling
     (Before going outside, I had no idea that it had been raining).

【ぽつぽつ】   Raining lightly; sprinkling
Ex. ぽつぽつと雨が降り出したけど、まだ傘は必要ないと思う。
     It started sprinkling, but I don't think I'll need an umbrella.

【ぱらぱら】   Rain that is a little heavier than "ぽつぽつ(sprinkling)", and is falling hard enough to make a light sound.
Ex. ぱらぱらと雨が降ってきたから、急いで家に帰った。
     The rain started coming down a bit, so I hurried home.

【ざあざあ】   Out of all of the different types of rainfall, this describes the strongest and heaviest kind.
Ex. ざあざあと滝のように雨が降っている。
     The rain is coming down like a waterfall.

◆   Level of strength from weakest to strongest; しとしと, ぽつぽつ, ぱらぱら, ざあざあ.

◆   "ぽつぽつ" and "ぱらぱら" are often used to describe rain when it begins falling.

Now that that is out of the way, we can continue on our こと-adventure.

II. Using 「ことがある/ない」 to talk about past experiences
(or the lack thereof)

This grammar structure was touched on in the previous section and also had an entire chapter devoted to it in my first book, so I won't spend too much time on it, but I thought it was worth going over again quickly because it really is, in my opinion, an absolutely necessary concept to have down. And now that we are familiar with nominalization and how it works, this structure should be quite simple to grasp.

Whenever we want to talk about the existence or non-existence of some action in the past, we can use 「〜ことがある」 or 「〜ことがない,」 respectively. The formation of this structure looks like this:

た-form verb + ことがある・ことがない

As you can see, all we have to do is simply conjugate a verb to its た-form and append 「ことがある」 if the experience exists, or 「ことがない」 if the experience does *not* exist. If you are unfamiliar with how to do this, I suggest going back to your favorite textbook (perhaps mine...) for a little review. Anyway, let's look at some example sentences:

1. 寿司を食べたことがない。
   I have never eaten sushi before.

2. 彼と会ったことがある。
   I have met him before.

3. あの映画を観たことがない。
   I have never seen that movie before.

4. スタバに行ったことがありますか？
   Have you ever been to Starbucks before?

5

→Answer: P233

（　　　　）内の単語を使って、1つの文を作りなさい。

Translate the following sentences into Japanese.

(1) I have never eaten tempura.（てんぷら / 食べる）

_____ 。

(2) Have you ever been to Japan?（日本 / 行く）

_____ ?

(3) Have you ever played this game before?（ゲーム / する）

_____ ?

(4) Have you read this book before?（本 / 読む）

_____ ?

(5) I have never read that book before.（本 / 読む）

_____ 。

III. Making decisions with 「ことにする」

Another useful grammar structure with 「こと」 is to describe making the decision to do or to *not* do something. The structure is very simple, and looks something like this:

> **Dictionary/ない-form verb ＋ ことにする**

As you can see, we just append 「ことにする」 to the dictionary-form or ない-form of our verb, and we get "to decide to [verb]" or "decide not to [verb.]"

It is important to remember, however, that the 「する」 in 「ことにする」 is in its dictionary-form, and as such can be conjugated like any dictionary-form verb.

Let's check out a few examples:

1. ハワイに引っ越しすることにした。
   I decided to move to Hawaii.

2. 彼のパーティーに行かないことにしました。
   I decided not to go to his party.

3. 留学することにしますか？
   Will you decide to study abroad?

4. 彼とデートしないことにする。
   I will choose to not go on a date with him.

5. 新しいのを買うことにした。*
   I decided to buy a new one.

Some Guy's Pro-Tip

The character 「の」, which is used to show possession and to sometimes indicate that a question is being asked, can also function similarly to how we use 'one' in English. In the following example we can see 「車」 from line A being replaced by 「の」 in line B.

Ex. A: 新しい車を買った？
     B: うん、赤いのを買った。（うん、赤い車を買った）

Ex. A: Did you buy a new car?
     B: Yeah, I bought a red one. (Yeah, I bought a red car.)

IV. "There is no need to ～" with 「ことはない」

Another really useful grammar structure with 「こと」 is describing something as being unnecessary to do. To form this structure, we simply couple 「ことはない」 with the dictionary-form of our verb.

> **Dictionary-form verb ＋ 「ことはない」**

Let's look at a few example sentences:

1. 謝^{あやま}ることはないよ。
   There is no need to apologize.

2. 迎^{むか}えに来^きてくれることはない。一人^{ひとり}で行^いける。
   There is no need to come to pick me up. I can go by myself.

3. お前は払^{まえ}^{はら}うことはないよ。彼^{かれ}の誘^{さそ}いだったから。*
   There is no need for you to pay. After all, it was his invitation.
   (He is the one who invited you.)

4. ご飯^{はん}を作^{つく}ってくれることはないよ。自分^{じぶん}で出来^で^きるから。
   It is not necessary for you to cook for me. I can do it myself.

Some Guy's Pro-Tip

「お前^{まえ}」 is a casual form of the word 「あなた」. It is typically used by men to refer to someone with whom they have a close relationship, or to someone who is of a lower social status than they are. My friends always get a kick out of it when I use this word, but just make sure not to call your boss, or someone like your friend's father 「お前^{まえ}」, or you might seriously offend them. You might want to avoid calling your girlfriend 「お前^{まえ}」 as well, as some ladies find it particularly offensive. Use with caution!

V. Talking about habits with 「ことにしている」

When we want to talk about a habit, or something we choose to do of our own volition, we can use this structure to express this idea. The structure looks like this:

> **Dictionary / ない-form verb ＋ ことにしている**

Let's check out a few example sentences:

1. 健康のため、毎日運動することにしている。
   For my health, I exercise everyday.

2. 寝る前に、本を読むことにしている。
   Before going to sleep, I always read a book.

3. 家の中で、うちのお父さんはタバコを吸わないことにしている。
   My father makes it a habit of not smoking in the house.

4. 学校から帰ってきたら、宿題をすることにしている。
   When I come home from school, I always do my homework.

5. 彼女は肉を食べないことにしている。ベジタリアンだから。
   She's a vegetarian, so she doesn't eat meat.

6. 健康のため、ファーストフードを食べないことにしている。
   For my heath, I don't eat fast food. (I choose not to eat fast food.)

As the 「る」 at the end of 「している」 should indicate to you, we aren't limited to only talking about the present. We can also conjugate 「している」 to the past tense, if we wanted to talk about something we *used* to do.

7. 健康のため、毎日運動することにしていた。
   For my health, I used to exercise everyday.

8. 家の中で、うちのお父さんはタバコを吸わないことにしていた。
   My father used to not be in the habit of smoking in the house.

9. 彼女は肉を食べないことにしていた。ベジタリアンだったから。
   She used to be a vegetarian, so she used to not eat meat.

9

VI. Talking about things that were decided regardless of our opinions, with 「ことになっている」

I really would have liked to have given this sub-topic a more concise title, but I couldn't think of a better way to put it. Whereas, as we just learned, 「ことにしている」 is used to talk about decisions we ourselves make, 「ことになっている」 is used to talk about things that were decided or determined by someone else, whether we like it or not. Let's look at an example sentence to help clarify:

Ex. 学校では、日本語しか話せないことになっている。*

We are only allowed to speak Japanese at school.

In this example, we can imagine that the speaker is attending some school where the only language they are allowed to speak is Japanese. This is a rule that was set by the school, and the speaker, most likely a student, had absolutely no say in the matter.

I like to think of the structure this way; 「なっている」 is the conjugated form of the verb 「なる」, which means "to become." Given what we know about nominalization, we can see that this structure roughly translates to "has become (and still is) 〜." So, 「日本語しか話せないことになっている」 could literally be translated as something like, "It has become that only Japanese can be spoken."

The structure of our sentence is the same as before:

Dictionary/ ない-form verb ＋ ことになっている

Let's look at a few more example sentences to help clear up any confusion:

1. 仕事のため、カナダに引っ越すことになっている。
   I have to move to Canada for work.

2. アメリカでは、１８歳未満は投票できないことになっている。
   In America, those who are under 18 years of age cannot vote.

3. 次の試合に負けたら帰ることになる。
   If I lose the next match, I will have to go back home.

4. 彼女とここで会うことになっていたが、いない。どこにいるだろう？
   I was supposed to meet with her here, but she's nowhere to be found. Where could she be?

5. 日本では車が道路の左側を走ることになっている。
   In Japan, they drive on the left side of the road.

Some Guy's Pro-Tip

A common mistake people make when first learning Japanese is to think that the ている -form of a verb equals the ing-form of a verb in English. While this idea seems to work most of the time, it cannot be applied to all cases.

We can of course say 「彼は本を読んでいる、」 if we wanted to say "He is reading a book," but when talking about the *state* or *condition* of something, 〜ている does *not* mean the subject is in the process of *doing* the action. I will give the very sentence that taught me this difference when I was first learning:

Ex. 彼は死んでいる。

How would you translate this sentence? At first glance, since 「死ぬ」 is the verb for 'to die,' a fitting translation seems to be "He is dying," but that would not be correct. The correct translation would be "He is dead." If we were to say 「彼は死んだ、」 that would translate to "He died." And if we were to say 「彼は死ぬ、」 that would translate to "He will die." 「死んでいる、」 however, does not talk about the *act* of dying, but the state of having died, that is to say 'being dead.'

So, when we have a sentence like 「学校では、日本語しか話せないことになっている、」 it does not mean that the rule at the school is *becoming* this way (and therefore still is not this way). It already *is* this way.

Japanese Onomatopoeia – "Warm"

【ぽかぽか】 Warm and toasty; comfortable feeling
Ex. 温泉につかると、体がぽかぽかする。
My whole body feels toasty warm after a soak in the hot spring.

【ほかほか】 When food or your body is at a perfect temperature.
Ex. 毎朝、ほかほかのお味噌汁を飲みます。
Every morning, I have a warm bowl of miso soup with my breakfast.

【かんかん】 The sun is very strong; feels very hot
Ex. アリゾナの夏の時期は、日がかんかんと照りつけている。
During the summer months in Arizona, the sun is blazing.

Now that we have finished our little crash course on nominalization and using 「こと」 with various structures, let's finish of this chapter with some quick review.

PRACTICE!

→Answer: P233

最も適切なものを1つ選びなさい。

Choose the right "こと-phrase" to fill in the blanks.

(6) I have never studied Chinese before.

中国語を勉強＿＿＿＿＿＿＿。

a. することはない　　b. したことがない　　c. したこと　　d. することにする

(7) I go to the gym every day. (because I want to stay healthy)

毎日ジムに行く＿＿＿＿＿＿＿。

a. ことになっている　　b. ことはない　　c. ことにした　　d. ことにしている

(8) I will not forget what he said.

彼が＿＿＿＿＿＿＿を忘れない。

a. 言ったこと　　b. 言うことはない　　c. 言うことにする　　d. 言ったことがある

(9) I cook breakfast every morning. (of my own volition)

毎朝、朝ご飯を作る＿＿＿＿＿＿＿。

a. ことになっている　　b. ことにしている　　c. ことはない　　d. ことにする

(10) There's no need to get angry.

怒る＿＿＿＿＿＿＿よ。

a. ことにする　　b. ことがある　　c. ことはない　　d. ことにしている

(11) Doing it by yourself must have been hard, huh.

一人で＿＿＿＿＿＿＿大変だったね。

a. やることは　　b. やったことがある　　c. やることにする　　d. やることはない

(12) She has lived abroad before.

彼女は海外に＿＿＿＿＿＿＿があります。

a. 住むことにした　　b. 住んだこと　　c. 住むこと　　d. 住むことに

(13) I have to work on Christmas. (because my boss told me to)

クリスマスに 働かないといけない＿＿＿＿＿＿。

    a. ことはない　　b. ことがある　　c. ことになっている　　d. ことにした

(14) I decided to buy the blue one.

青のを＿＿＿＿＿＿。

    a. 買うことはない　　b. 買ったことがある　　c. 買うこと　　d. 買うことにした

(15) There's no need to cry. It's okay.

＿＿＿＿＿＿ないよ。大丈夫だよ。

    a. 泣いたことが　　b. 泣くことは　　c. 泣くことにし　　d. 泣いたこと

(16) I decided to buy this book.

この本を＿＿＿＿＿＿。

    a. 買うことにした　　b. 買うこと　　c. 買ったことがある　　d. 買うことはない

(17) You cannot ride in airplanes with your dogs.

ペットの犬と飛行機に乗れない＿＿＿＿＿＿。

    a. ことはない　　b. ことになっている　　c. ことにした　　d. ことがある

13

Chapter Summary

✧ Nominalization is the act of turning something that is not a noun such as a verb-phrase into a noun

✧ We can pair 「こと」 with the informal past-tense-form of a verb to talk about the existence or non-existence of an experience

✧ We can pair 「こと」 with 「にする」 to talk about making decisions

✧ We can pair 「こと」 with the ない-form of a verb to talk about that action being unnecessary

✧ We can pair 「こと」 with 「にしている」 when we want to talk about something we do as a habit, or of our own volition

✧ We can pair 「こと」 with 「になっている」 when we want to talk about something that was decided by someone else

✧ い and な-adjectives can also be nominalized

✧ When coupling a な-adjective in its dictionary-form with 「こと」 we must append 「な」 immediately after the な-adjective

Chapter 2
「～てほしい / もらいたい」
Need you to ～

Another useful ability to have is to be able to talk about what you (or someone else) would like someone to do. We can use ～てほしい or ～てもらいたい for this purpose.

Before we get too far into this chapter, however, I feel that a brief description of the い-adjective 「ほしい」 is in order.

What most people find confusing about the word 「ほしい」 is that, although it is an adjective, its meaning often translates to 'want,' which is, of course, a verb. Don't confuse yourself, though. Just remember that 「ほしい」 is an adjective, and should be used as such. If it helps, instead of thinking that 「ほしい」 means 'want,' think of it as meaning something like, "is wanted," giving it an adjectival quality of 'being wanted.'

The use of 「ほしい」 to describe something that is wanted or desired can also seem a little tricky at first, but it is really quite easy. The object of desire does not take the particle 「を.」 Instead, it takes 「が.」 If you can commit those last two sentences to memory, then you should have no problems mastering this useful adjective.

Let's check out a few example sentences. The structure will look something like this (keep in mind that in casual Japanese, the subject of the sentence and 「です」 are often omitted):

> **(Subject ＋ は) ＋ Object ＋ が ＋ ほしい**

1. 私は新しい靴がほしいです。
   I want new shoes.

2. あれがほしい。
   I want that.

3. 彼女は赤いのがほしい。
   She wants the red one.

4. あの背が高い人はもっと大きな車がほしい。*
   That tall person over there wants a bigger car.

Some Guy's Pro-Tip

The い-adjective 「大きい」 can also be used as a な-adjective. For all intents and purposes, their meanings are the exact same. The above example sentence may also have been written as:

あの背が高い人はもっと大きい車がほしい。

That tall person over there wants a bigger car.

As you can see, using the い-adjective 「大きい」 does not change the meaning of the sentence. Both are perfectly fine. I find, however, that when describing the object of a sentence as being 'big,' the な-adjective form is more common. For instance,

Ex. 大きな犬がほしい。

I want a big dog.

The 'dog' is the object of my desire, and as such I decided to describe it using the な-adjective form. If, however, I wanted to simply describe the physical characteristic of the subject of a sentence, I would use the い-adjective form.

Ex. 僕の犬は大きい。

My dog is big.

In this sentence, since I'm just describing 'my dog' (the subject of the sentence), I simply use the い-adjective form.

This quirky little detail also applies to 「小さい」, the word for 'small/little'

Ex. 小さな犬がほしい。

I want a little dog.

Ex. 僕の犬は小さい。

My dog is small.

If you truly have a grasp of what was taught in my first book, then you will no doubt have already realized that as an い-adjective, we can conjugate 「ほしい」 in a number of ways:

5. 私は新しい靴はほしくないです。
   I do not want new shoes.

6. あれはほしくなかった。
   I didn't want that.

7. 彼女は赤いのがほしかった。
   She wanted the red one.

8. あの背が高い人がもっと大きな車がほしかったら、買ってあげるよ。
   If that tall person over there wants a bigger car, I will buy him one.

As you can see, as an い-adjective in its dictionary-form, we can conjugate 「ほしい」 to the negative-form, the negative-past-tense form, the past-tense-form, and even the conditional-form. If you are not comfortable doing these kinds of conjugations, make sure to go back and review a little before moving on too far.

Now try a few yourself. Translate the following sentences by unscrambling the given words:

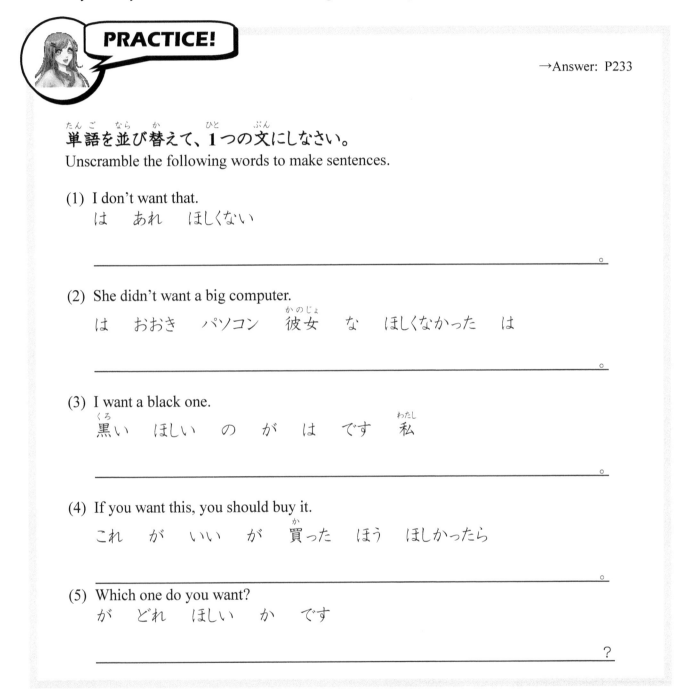

PRACTICE!

→Answer: P233

たん ご なら か ひと ぶん
単語を並び替えて、1つの文にしなさい。
Unscramble the following words to make sentences.

(1) I don't want that.
は　あれ　ほしくない

_____。

(2) She didn't want a big computer.
は　おおき　パソコン　彼女(かのじょ)　な　ほしくなかった　は

_____。

(3) I want a black one.
黒(くろ)い　ほしい　の　が　は　です　私(わたし)

_____。

(4) If you want this, you should buy it.
これ　が　いい　が　買(か)った　ほう　ほしかったら

_____。

(5) Which one do you want?
が　どれ　ほしい　か　です

_____？

17

Before moving on to the next part of this chapter, it is also worth mentioning that 「が」 isn't the *only* particle you will see being used with 「ほしい」 in this way. 「も」 is also often coupled with 「ほしい.」 For example:

9. これもほしい。
   I also want this.

10. 大きくないものもほしい。
    I also want one that is not big.

11. 新しい靴もほしかったですか？
    Did you also want new shoes?

Now that all of that is out of the way, we can get back to the main point of this chapter; using ～て ほしい and ～てもらいたい.

This grammar structure is used to express what we want someone to do. Our sentence structure will look something like this:

Subject + は + **Object 1** + に + **(Object 2)** + **て-verb** + ほしい/もらいたい

Let's check out a few examples sentences to help make this clear:

12. 私は彼にアイスを買ってほしいです。
    I want him to buy ice-cream.

13. 両親に長生きしてもらいたいと思う。
    I want my parents to live a long time.

14. あなたに一人でやってほしい。
    I want you to do it by yourself.

15. 彼女にオムレツを作ってもらいたい。
    I want her to make an omelet for me.

16. 彼に帰ってほしい。
    I want him to go home.

Naturally, we aren't restricted to solely using 〜てほしい/もらいたい in their dictionary forms. As い -adjectives, we can conjugate them a number of ways.

17. 私は彼にアイスを買ってほしかったです。
I wanted him to buy ice cream.

18. 両親に長生きしてほしくない。
I don't want my parents to live a long time. (Don't worry Mom and Dad, it's just an example)

19. あなたに一人でやってほしくなかった。
I didn't want you to do it by yourself.

20. 彼女にオムレツを作ってもらいたかったら、頼んでみなきゃ。
If I want her to make me an omelet I have to ask.

21. 彼に帰ってほしかった。
I wanted him to go home.

Now you may be asking what the difference is between 〜てほしい and 〜てもらいたい. The simple explanation is that they are the same. Both mean the exact same thing. Though, 〜てもらいたい should be used in more formal situations, as it is considered to be more polite.

擬音語 **Japanese Onomatopoeia – "Movement 1"**

【てきぱき】　Quick and efficient; Take care of something in an efficient manner
Ex. 彼女はてきぱきと家の片付けをした。
She cleaned up the house in a flash.

【もたもた】　Slow, inefficient; To take time in doing something
Ex. もたもたと準備をしていたから、バスに乗り遅れた。
I was slow in getting ready, so I missed the bus.

【のろのろ】　To move extremely slow like tortoise.
Ex. のろのろ運転をしていると、後ろの車からクラクションを鳴らされた。
When I was driving at a snail's pace the car behind me honked its horn.

Let's finish off this chapter with some translation practice.

→Answer: P233

（　　　　）内の単語を使って、1つの文を作りなさい。

Translate the following sentences into Japanese.

(6) I want her to buy a dog. （犬 / 買う）

_____。

(7) I don't want her to go. （彼女 / 行く）

_____。

(8) I didn't want my older brother to come home. （お兄ちゃん / 帰る）

_____。

(9) He wanted me to make breakfast. （私 / 朝ごはん）

_____。

(10) I wanted them to win. （彼ら / 勝つ）

_____。

(11) Do you want me to write it? （僕 / 書く）

_____？

(12) I want my parents to visit Japan. （両親 / 来日する）

_____。

Chapter Summary

✧ 「ほしい」 is an い-adjective that is used to describe something that is wanted

✧ The particle 「が」 is used to mark the object of desire. 「も」 may also be used

✧ 「大_{おお}きい」 and 「小_{ちい}さい」 can be expressed as な-adjectives; 「大_{おお}きな」 and 「小_{ちい}さな」

✧ We can couple 「ほしい」 or 「もらいたい」 with a て-verb to express the desire of wanting someone to do something

✧ 「〜てほしい」 and 「〜てもらいたい」 have the same meaning, but 「〜てもらいたい」 is a more polite

✧ The person that we want to do the action is marked by 「に」

☺ I love my parents and 長生_{ながい}きしてもらいたいと思_{おも}います。

Chapter 3
Using 「か」 to combine sentences and make statements

Of course, we are already familiar with how to use 「か」 when asking questions; e.g. 何時に来ますか？ In this chapter, however, we are going to take a look at how to use this normally question-asking-particle to make statements.

This usage of 「か」 that we are going to learn basically takes two sentences and makes them into one. Let's look at an example:

Ex: 私は彼が何時に来るか分かりません。

I don't know what time he is going to come.

Let's break this sentence down a bit, shall we? I mentioned before that this usage of 「か」 combines two sentences into one. So, what did the two original sentences look like, you wonder?

Ex: 彼は何時に来ますか？私は分かりません。

What time is he coming? I don't know.

This helps exemplify where the usage of 「か」 comes from. Anytime where we see 「か」 being used to combine two sentences into one, we are bound to find some sort of question-asking-word; いつ, なんで, 何, どこ, 誰, etc...

Let's take a look at a few more examples:

1. 何で彼がそんなことを知っているのか？私は知りません。

   How does he know that? I don't know.

   → 何で彼がそんなことを知っている<u>か</u>知りません。

   I don't know how he knows that.

2. いつクラスが始まりますか？それが書いてありますか？

   When will class start? Is that written down?

   → いつクラスが始まる<u>か</u>書いてありますか？

   Is when class will start written down?

3. 彼女はどこにバッグを置きましたか？私は覚えていません。

   Where did she put the bag? I don't remember.

   → 彼女がどこにバッグを置いたか覚えていません。

   I don't remember where she put the bag.

4. 彼の一番好きな俳優さんは誰ですか？あなたは知っていますか？

   Who is his favorite actor? Do you know?

   → 彼の一番好きな俳優さんは誰か知っていますか？

   Do you know who his favorite actor is?

5. 何のために日本に行きますか？教えてくれますか？

   Why are you going to Japan? Will you tell me?

   → 何のために日本に行くか教えてくれますか？

   Will you tell me why you are going to Japan?

擬音語 Japanese Onomatopoeia – "Movement 2"

【ぐずぐず】 Lackadaisical, to act without purpose; to take time in making a decision
Ex. 「ぐずぐずしないで、早くどのランチを注文するか決めてよ。」
"Quit dawdling! Hurry up and choose what you want to order for lunch."

【そろそろ】 To move slowly and quietly.
Ex. 赤ちゃんが起きないように、お母さんはそろそろと歩いて部屋を出た。
So as not to wake the baby, the mother tip-toed out of the room.

【いそいそ】 Jumping up and down with joy or in anticipation
Ex. クリスマスの朝、子ども達はいそいそとプレゼントがあるツリーの下に集まってきた。
On Christmas morning, the children excitedly gathered under the Christmas tree with all of the presents.

PRACTICE!

→Answer: P233

「か」を使って、2つの文を1つの文にしなさい。

Take the following sentences and combine them into one, using 「か」.

(1) お父さんは何時に帰りますか？あなたは知っていますか？

What time will Dad come home? Do you know?

_____ ？

(2) 何人来ますか？あなたは知っていますか？

How many people will come? Do you know?

_____ ？

(3) これは誰のですか？私は知りません。

Whose is this? I don't know.

_____ 。

(4) 何が書いてありますか？私は読めないです。

What is written here? I cannot read it.

_____ 。

(5) 彼の誕生日はいつですか？あなたは知っていますか？

When is his birthday? Do you know?

_____ ？

Chapter 4
「〜くらい / ぐらい」 About 〜

くらい/ぐらい are two useful "words" that can be used to express and describe a number of different things (I say "words" because they cannot stand by themselves as typical words can, but I'm not sure exactly what part of speech they would be considered...). They can be used with nouns, verbs, and adjectives. So, as you will see, they are quite versatile.

In this chapter, we will take a look at three common usages of this grammar structure.

First and perhaps the most commonly used application of くらい/ぐらい is to express the meaning of 'about,' or 'around,' as it pertains to some number or figure. Some example sentences will help clarify what I mean.

1. ここからオフィスまで15分<ruby>分<rt>じゅうごふん</rt></ruby>ぐらいだ。
   From here to my office takes about 15 minutes.

2. 今日<ruby><rt>きょう</rt></ruby>、1時間半<ruby><rt>いちじかんはん</rt></ruby>くらい運動<ruby><rt>うんどう</rt></ruby>をしていた。
   Today I exercised for about an hour and a half.

3. 5％<ruby><rt>ごぱーせんと</rt></ruby>くらいの日本人<ruby><rt>にほんじん</rt></ruby>はベジタリアンです。
   5% of Japanese people are vegetarians.

Some Guy's Pro-Tip

Grammatically speaking, there is no difference between using くらい or ぐらい. The only difference between the two is, obviously, pronunciation. So, use whichever one you like or is easier for you to say. You may find in some situations that the hard ぐ sound 'flows' better than the soft く, and vice-versa.

Next, くらい/ぐらい can also be used to express the *degree* of something.

4. もう歩けない<ruby>歩<rt>ある</rt></ruby>くらい足<ruby><rt>あし</rt></ruby>が痛<ruby><rt>いた</rt></ruby>い。
   My foot hurts so bad I can't walk anymore.

5. この本は悲しくて泣いてしまうぐらいだ。
This book is sad enough to make me cry.

6. 彼くらいの背の高さなら、俺も絶対にダンクシュートできるよ。
If I were as tall as him, I'd definitely be able to dunk too, man.

And the last usage we'll look it is quite similar to the previous one, albeit a little more tricky to understand. It is also used to describe the degree of something, but from that something's 'lowest extreme.' And don't worry if that last part was difficult to understand, take a look at the following sentences, and then I will attempt to clarify.

7. かぜくらいで学校を休めない。
I can't skip school just because I have a little cold.

8. 運動する前にストレッチするぐらいの時間はあるはずだ。
Before exercising, you should at least have the time to stretch a bit.

9. そんなことを知らないのは俺ぐらいだ。
I'm just about the only person who wouldn't know something like that.

If we look at the first sentence, we can see what I mean by 'lowest extreme.'

かぜ is the word used to describe a cold or a minor sickness (かぜ also means 'wind,' which is where the connection with an illness derives. Perhaps you caught a cold while you were outside without a coat?).

Anyway, the student speaking this sentence is expressing that a simple cold is not enough to justify taking a day off of school. Perhaps if they had the flu or a high fever, then it would be okay. But *just* a little cold?

By using くらい, they are expressing that a cold is not a big deal, which is what I meant earlier when I said 'lowest extreme.' A sickness can be life-threateningly severe or a minor nuisance; two extremes. This usage of くらい focuses on the 'minor' or 'low' extreme.

In the example sentence 8, we can see the same logic. Perhaps the trainer speaking these words thinks that stretching is very important, and that no matter how busy or pressed for time you are, you *at the very least* have a couple of minutes to stretch, as if to say "You can't be so pressed for time that you don't have a few minutes to stretch before working out."
And that's going to do it for this chapter, lets recap really quickly what we learned:

Chapter Summary

✧ くらい/ぐらい can be used to express 'about' or 'around' when talking about a figure, or the degree of something

✧ They can be appended to nouns, verbs, and adjectives

✧ The only difference between くらい and ぐらい is pronunciation

Chapter 5
「〜だらけ」
Covered in 〜; 〜 everywhere

This chapter is going to be short and sweet, but it explains how to use a commonly used grammar structure. Typically, 〜だらけ is used to convey a negative feeling about a thing or situation. Its use is quite simple, though. We just have to place it after a noun to express that there is "too much [noun]."

Let's look at a couple of example sentences to help illustrate. The noun and だらけ will be underlined.

1. 彼の部屋はほこりだらけです。
   His room is covered in dust.

2. 僕の試験は間違いだらけだった。どうしよう…。
   My test was full of mistakes. What am I going to do…?

3. 彼の部屋は漫画だらけで、足の踏み場もないくらい。
   His room is full of so much manga, that there is hardly a place to step.

4. 「しわだらけのシャツを着るな！」
   "Don't wear a shirt that is all wrinkled up!"

5. 長崎が大好きです！いい人だらけです！
   I love Nagasaki! It's chock-full of good/nice people!

It is also important to note that when we want to use 〜だらけ to modify a noun, we must connect the two with the particle 「の」.

6. 泥だらけの靴
   Shoes covered in mud (mud-covered shoes)

7. 血だらけの患者
   A (medical) patient covered in blood (a blood-covered patient)

Some Guy's Pro-Tip

While mostly used for talking about something in a negative way, as we can see in example sentence 5, 「だらけ」 can also be used to express something positive such as "full of good people."

Now let's finish off the lesson with a little だらけ practice. Remember, it will always proceed the noun it is describing as being excessive/overabundant.

→Answer: P234

単語を並び替えて、1つの文にしなさい。
Unscramble the following words to make sentences.

(1) My cat came home all beat up.

傷　うち　猫　だらけ　に　帰って　の　が　なって　きた

_____。

(2) I am unable to read a newspapers that are full of Kanji.

は　新聞　漢字　私　読めない　だらけ　の　を　です

_____。

(3) My brother's room is full of trash/garbage.

弟　部屋　は　ゴミ　の　だらけ　です

_____。

(4) He doesn't brush his teeth, so his teeth are full of cavities.

虫歯　歯　彼　は　磨かない　だらけ　です　から　を

_____。

(5) My homework had a ton of mistakes.

でした　私　は　間違い　の　だらけ　宿題

_____。

29

Chapter 6
Placing the blame with 「～せい」 and 「せいか」

There are many reasons one learns another language. Some people study a foreign language to enrich their cultural understanding of the world. Others do so in order to land a high-paying job, or perhaps to try and make the world a better place. But one aspect that I think often gets overlooked when it comes to mastering another tongue is gaining the ability to blame others for things (that you may be responsible for anyway)!

In order to place the blame for a particular incident on someone or something, we are going to look at two grammar structures that serve this purpose.

First, we'll look at using ～せい.

We use ～せい when we want to place the blame *squarely* on someone (even ourselves) or something. This grammar structure can be used with nouns, verbs, い-adjectives, and な-adjectives. I trust that if have made it this far into my series, it shouldn't be necessary to point out how the different parts-of-speech (nouns, verbs, adjectives) determine how ～せい is used, but I will give a quick explanation anyway, and ask that as you read the following example sentences you make a note of what part-of-speech せい is being used in conjunction with.

Noun + の
Verb
い-adjective
な-adjective + な ⎫ + せい

1. 彼のせいでみんなが怒っている。
   Because of him, everyone is angry.

2. チケットを失くしたせいで、スタジアムに入れなかったんだ。
   Because I lost the tickets, we couldn't get into the stadium.

3. 景気があまりよくないせいで、今年はボーナスがないそうだ。
   Due to the bad economy, there is no bonus this year.

4. 設計が複雑なせいで、サクラダファミリアはなかなか完成しない。

Because the design plan is so complicated, Sagrada Familia is not likely to be completed any time soon.

5. 電車に間に合わなかったのを僕のせいにするの？お前のせいだろう！

You're blaming *me* for missing the train? It was *your* fault!

Now we'll look at using 〜せいか.

This structure is used when we want to blame someone/something, but we aren't completely confident that it is true. The reason we are giving is more of a guess based on some kind of evidence. Let's check out a few example sentences.

6. たくさんの仕事をしたせいか、かぜを引いてしまった。

I probably caught a cold from working too hard.

7. 天気のせいか、今日はちょっと元気がない。

I don't know if it is because of the weather or what, but I am just not feeling 100% today.

8. 食べ過ぎたせいか、ズボンがきついです。

Maybe my pants are tight because I ate so much.

9. 空気がきれいなせいか、深呼吸をすると気持ちがいい。

Maybe it's the fresh air, but whenever I took a deep breath it feels so good.

10. 気のせいか、最近田中さんは気が短いね。

Lately I feel like Mr. Tanaka has a bad temper/is quick to get angry.

As you can see, 〜せいか differs from 〜せい in that the cause for a problem isn't completely certain. In example sentence 6, for instance, the person is saying that got sick from working too much, but they can't be 100% sure that is the reason. Or, in example sentence 7, the speaker is blaming the weather for their lack of energy. It could be because of any number of things, but the most likely culprit is the bad weather, so they use 〜せいか to express this.

「せい」か「せいか」を使って、2つの文章を1つの文章にしなさい。

Take the following sentences and combine them into one, using 「せい」 or 「せいか」.

(1) 祭りがある。人が多い。

So many people must be here because of the festival.

_____。

(2) 私は寝不足でした。映画館で寝てしまった。

I must have fallen asleep at the movie theater because I haven't been sleeping well lately.

_____。

(3) 建物が古い。歩くと床がきしむ。

Because the building is old, the floor creaks when you walk.

_____。

(4) 彼女は真面目。時々冗談が通じない。

Because she is so serious, sometimes jokes go over her head.

_____。

(5) 彼は先生に怒られた。彼はしょんぼりしている。

He's feeling down because the teacher got mad at him.

_____。

(6) 寝坊をした。電車に乗り遅れた。

I overslept, so I missed the train.

_____。

Chapter 7
「〜みたいだ」 Appears to be 〜

We can use this structure for a number of purposes. One common usage is to express that something seems or looks a certain way.

This structure can be used with nouns, verbs, い-adjectives, and な-adjectives (or as a stand-alone expression).

1. あのカフェは人気がないみたいだね。いつもすいている。
   That café doesn't seem to very popular. It's always empty.

2. 田中先生はすごく怒っているみたいだから、明日彼女にこの質問を聞いてみよう。
   Mrs. Tanaka looks to be quite angry (now), so I'll ask her this question tomorrow.

3. ヤバイ、かぜを引いたみたいだ。薬を買いに行かないといけない。
   Oh no, I seem to have caught a cold. I need to go buy some medicine.

4. 「明日、田中くんもパーティーに来るそうだ。」
   「うん、みたいだね。一人で来るかな。」
   "I heard that Tanaka is also coming to the party tomorrow."
   "Yeah, so it seems. I wonder if he'll come by himself."

We can also use 〜みたい with a noun or a verb to express that something only *seems* a certain way, but in reality is not (that way).

5. ＪＬＰＴ一級に合格した！本当に夢みたいだ！
   I passed the Level 1 JLPT! It's like I'm dreaming!

6. ジャガイモも食べないの？好き嫌いが多いね。子供みたいだ。
   You don't eat/like potatoes either? You're picky about your food. You're like a child.

7. やっぱり今日は寒いね。10月なのに。もう冬が来たみたいだ。
   Man it's cold today! And it's only October. It's as if winter has already come.

We can also use 〜みたい in conjunction with a noun when we want to give an example.

---

8. 僕は寒がり屋さんだから、沖縄みたいなところで暮らしたいな。

I can't stand the cold, so I want to live in a warm place like Okinawa.

9. トムさんみたいに日本語を話せるようになりたいです。頑張ります！

I want to be able to speak Japanese as well as Tom. I can do it!

10. 彼みたいに日本語を勉強しないと、上手にならないよ。

If you don't study Japanese like him (as he does), you won't become good at it.

In example sentences 1-4, we can see that the speakers are basically conjecturing about what they feel the truth to be. They aren't sure, but they are confident in the feelings/assertion. In the example sentence 1, for instance, the speaker can surmise that the cafe is not popular based on evidence (it's always empty). And in example sentence 2, the speaker can tell by Mrs. Tanaka's expression or body language that she is upset/angry about something, and feels that it would be better to talk to her tomorrow about her question.

In example sentences 5-8, the speakers are expressing how something looks/seems/sounds/feels, but they know that it's not the reality of the situation. In example sentence 5, the speaker is so surprised by the fact that they passed the JLPT that it feels like a dream. Of course, they know it is not. Or in example sentence 7, the speaker knows that winter has not come, and that it is definitely still fall, but it's so cold that it is as if winter came early.

And in example sentences 8-10, we can see that we are pairing 〜みたい with a noun to use that noun as an example. In example sentence 9, the speaker feels that Tom speaks Japanese really well, and hopes that one day they will be able to speak "like Tom."

Some Guy's Pro-Tip

What's the difference between 「みたい」 and 「ようだ」?

Some of you may be wondering what the difference between this structure and 「ようだ／ように」 is. For example, we could very well say:

Ex. トムのように日本語を話せるようになりたいです。

The two structures are essentially the same, but you'll often find that 「みたい」 is used more in casual conversation. Also, please notice the の after our noun トム. It must be included.

→Answer: P234

（　　　　　）に「くらい/ぐらい」か「みたい」を入れなさい。

Fill in the (   )'s with either「くらい/ぐらい」or「みたい」

(1) The kid is sleeping all curled up like a cat.

子供<small>こども</small>が猫<small>ねこ</small>（　　　　　　　）に丸<small>まる</small>まって寝<small>ね</small>ている。

(2) I would like to help, but I am only able to do this much.

力<small>ちから</small>になりたいけど、私<small>わたし</small>にはこれ（　　　　　　　）しかできない。

(3) I'll be ready in about 15 minutes.

あと15分<small>じゅうごふん</small>（　　　　　　　）で準備<small>じゅんび</small>ができます。

(4) Mom seems to be in high spirits. I wonder if something good happened.

お母<small>かあ</small>さんは機嫌<small>きげん</small>がいい（　　　　　　　）。何<small>なに</small>かいいことがあったのかな。

(5) You were able to at least call, right? I was worried when I didn't hear from you.

電話<small>でんわ</small>をする（　　　　　　　）はできたでしょう？連絡<small>れんらく</small>がなくて心配<small>しんぱい</small>していたんだよ。

(6) That employee over there doesn't seem busy. They are just playing on their phone.

あのスタッフは暇<small>ひま</small>（　　　　　　　）で、ずっと携帯<small>けいたい</small>をいじっている。

(7) If only I were as tall as he is.

彼<small>かれ</small>（　　　　　　　）身長<small>しんちょう</small>が高<small>たか</small>かったら良<small>よ</small>かったのに。

(8) It seems that there is some fun even going on in the park today, wanna go check it out?

今日<small>きょう</small>は公園<small>こうえん</small>で何<small>なに</small>か楽<small>たの</small>しいことがある（　　　　　　　）だから、行<small>い</small>ってみない？

Chapter 8
「〜つもり」 Thought I 〜

If you read the topic for this lesson and got a sense of Deja Vu, don't worry. In my first book, I covered how to use 〜つもり to talk about our plans (or those of others). But in this book, we are going to learn how to use 〜つもり to talk about something we *thought* was true (but in fact was not).

Using 〜つもり in this fashion can be a little complicated (grammatically speaking). So, I am going to lay out how to pair it with nouns, verbs, and adjectives.

> **Noun +** の
>
> **Verb [casual-past tense +** ている**-form]**
>
> い**-adjective**
>
> な**-adjective +** な
>
> **+** つもり

Let's look at some example sentences to give you a better idea. Please pay attention to the part-of-speech 「つもり」 is being paired with.

1. 教科書をリュックに入れたつもりだったが、教室で見たらなかった。
   どこにあるだろう…。
   I thought I put my textbook in my bag, but when I got to class, it wasn't in there.
   Where could it be?

2. 格好いいつもりでナンパしようとしたけど、ダメだった。もう彼氏がいると言われた。
   Thinking I was a cool guy, I tried hitting on the girl, but she rejected me.
   She said she already had a boyfriend.

3. 全部分かっているつもりでテストを受けたけど、全然できなかった。
   I took the test thinking I understood everything, but I totally bombed it.

4. 私は中国語が分かるつもりでこの小説を買ったけど、全然分からない。
   お金の無駄だった。
   I bought this book thinking my Chinese was good enough to understand it, but I don't understand it at all. It was just waste of money.

5. 冗談のつもりで言ったけど、彼女は超怒った。どうやって謝ればいいだろう。
    I said it as a joke, but she got *really* angry. I wonder how I can make it up to her.

In the first example sentence, we can see つもり being paired with the verb 入れた, to get something like, "thought I had put x in y." And in the second sentence, つもり is being paired with the い-adjective いい. In sentence three, we can see つもり being paired with a verb as well, but this time the verb is in the continuous ている-form. Please notice that we can append つもり as is and do not need any particles to connect the verb/adjectives together. However, in sentences 4 we can see つもり being paired with the な-adjective 上手, in which case we need to put な between the adjective and つもり. And in sentence 5, we can see つもり being paired with the noun 冗談 (joke) using の.

PRACTICE!

→Answer: P234

(   )に「つもり」か「ことにしている」を入れなさい。
Fill in the (   )'s with either「つもり」 or 「ことにしている」.

(1) I thought I left my house early enough, but I missed the bus.
    家を早く出た(   )だったけど、バスに乗り遅れた。

(2) I plan on working in Japan in the future.
    将来は日本で働く(   )です。

(3) I only meant to take a little nap, but I ended up falling into a deep sleep.
    少しだけの(   )だったが、うっかり熟睡してしまった。

(4) I am planning on studying abroad in Japan next year and am really looking forward to it.
    来年、日本に留学する(   )ので、今からとても楽しみだ。

(5) I went out shopping in order to buy my girlfriend a present.
    彼女へのプレゼントを買う(   )で、買い物にでかけた。

(6) I was invited by my friend, so I am planning on going out to a party this weekend.
    友達から誘われたから、今週末は友達のパーティーに行く(   )。

(7) I am planning on going out in my new shoes tomorrow. I hope it's sunny (and not rainy).
    明日は新しい靴で出かける(   )から、晴れるといいな。

37

Chapter 9
「〜らしい」 Seems 〜

This structure has a couple of usages. The first that we'll look at is as a way to describe what something "seems like," or to report some news or gossip that we have heard.

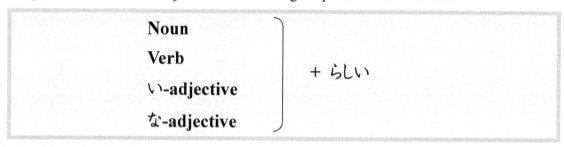

1. 明日は<u>雨らしい</u>。傘を忘れないで。
   I heard it's going to rain tomorrow. Don't forget your umbrella.

2. 今日、田中さんは来ないそうだ。風邪を<u>引いているらしい</u>。
   I hear that Tanaka isn't coming today. It seems he is feeling under the weather.

3. 明子さんは部屋に<u>いないらしい</u>。どこに行ったのだろうね。
   Akiko doesn't appear to be in her room. I wonder where she went.

4. 彼はやっと彼女が<u>できたらしい</u>。
   It seems that he finally found a girlfriend.

5. 長崎のちゃんぽんは<u>美味しいらしい</u>。食べたことある？
   Nagasaki's *chanpon* is really good, they say. Have you ever had it?

6. 佐藤さんについての噂は<u>本当らしい</u>。信じがたいね。
   That rumor about Mrs. Sato is true, they say. It's hard to believe.

7. 彼女はちょっと<u>変わっているらしい</u>。彼女と話すな。
   They say she is a little strange. Don't talk to her.

8. 人参を沢山食べたら、背が<u>伸びるらしい</u>。本当かな…。
   If you eat a lot of carrots, they say you'll grow taller. I wonder if that's really true…

9. その大学を卒業するのは<u>大変らしい</u>。
   Graduating from that college is supposed to be (said to be) difficult.

Odds are you are already familiar with using 「〜ようだ」, 「〜そうだ」, and 「〜みたいだ」 to express the same thing (reporting something we've heard or how something seems). So, you may be wondering "What's the difference between them and 「〜らしい」?" Well, the differences aren't too drastic. If we have the sentences...

10. ジェレミーは元気じゃない<u>らしい</u>。
I heard that Jeremy isn't feeling well.

11. ジェレミーは元気じゃない<u>そうだ</u>。
They say that Jeremy isn't feeling well.

12. ジェレミーは元気じゃない<u>みたいだ</u>。
Jeremy doesn't seem to be feeling well.

13. ジェレミーは元気じゃない<u>ようだ</u>。
Jeremy doesn't seem to be feeling well.

We can see from example sentences 10 and 11 that when we use 「〜らしい」 or 「〜そうだ」 that we are simply reporting something that we have *heard*; perhaps on television, or from a friend. When we use 「〜みたいだ」 or 「〜ようだ」, like in example sentences 12 and 13, we are basing our thoughts on our own assumptions. Maybe the speaker in sentences 12 and 13 saw Jeremy in person and he was pale, or his voice sounded scratchy, and they came to the conclusion that "he is not feeling well" on their own, based on this evidence.

As such, it should also be known that using 「〜らしい」 when you are talking about yourself is quite unnatural sounding. Instead of saying, 「私はかぜを引いたらしい」, it would be better to say 「私はかぜを引いたみたいだ」 Since 「〜らしい」 is used to report information we have heard from some outside source, 「私はかぜを引いたらしい」 would essentially translate to, "I heard that I have caught a cold," which is obviously odd, because you more than anyone should know whether you have caught a cold or not. 「私はかぜを引いたみたいだ」 would be more natural, as it would translate to, "It seems I have caught a cold," because maybe I have a temperature.

The second use of 「〜らしい」 that we are going to take a look at is to express a feeling that we get from something, or to express that something represents its own particular quality or characteristic.

Noun + らしい

---

14. もっと<u>学生らしく</u>しなさい！ちゃんと勉強しなさい！ゲームばかりしないで！

Act more like a student (how a student should act)! Study hard!
Don't just play games all day!

15. そんないいことをするなんて<u>彼らしい</u>ね。やっぱり、いい人だね。

Doing such a nice thing is just like him, isn't it. Yeah, he is a nice guy.

16. 時々かぜを引くけれど、<u>病気らしい</u>病気をしたことがない。

I catch a cold from time to time, but I've never had a serious illness before.

17. まだこんなに暑い。いつ<u>秋らしく</u>なるのかな…。

It's still so hot. When is it going to be more fall-like…

18. 彼は<u>男らしい</u>人だ。

He is a manly man.

19. 彼女はまだ幼いけど、全然<u>子供らしくない</u>。彼女と話せばすぐに分かる。

She is still young, but she is not childish (like a child) at all.
If you talk with her, you'll see what I mean.

20. こんなひどいことをするなんて、<u>あなたらしくない</u>。

To do such a terrible thing…this isn't like you at all.

たんご ならか ひとぶん
単語を並び替えて、1つの文にしなさい。
Unscramble the following words to make sentences.

(1) The cherry blossoms are blooming and spring has come.
　　はる　　　　　　　　　さ　　　　　　　　　　　　さくら
　　春　きたね　咲いて　が　なって　桜　らしく

　　_____。

(2) I hear that this story is scary.
　　こわ　　ほん　　　　　　　　　はなし
　　怖い　本　は　この　話　らしい　の

　　_____。

(3) It appears my cell phone has run out of battery power.
　　じゅうでん　　　　　　　　　　けいたい　き
　　充電　みたいだ　の　携帯　切れた　が

　　_____。

(4) According to the forecast, it is going to start raining this afternoon.
　　てんきよほう　　あめ　　　　　　　　　　　　ひる
　　天気予報　雨　によると　なる　に　昼　ようだ　から

　　_____。

(5) I hear that she drinks soy milk everyday.
　　まいにち　　　とうにゅう　　　　の　　　　　かのじょ
　　毎日　は　豆乳　らしい　飲んでいる　彼女　を

　　_____。

(6) I heard that, due to the rain, today's camping trip has been canceled.
　　きょう　　　　　　　　　　　ちゅうし　あめ
　　今日　は　キャンプ　だから　中止　雨　の　だ　そうだ

　　_____。

(7) They say that this app is useful.
　　　　べんり
　　は　便利　この　アプリ　らしい

　　_____。

Chapter 10
「〜のではないだろうか」
「〜のではないかと思う」
I would say that 〜; I feel that 〜

These next two structures are quite the mouthful, but they are useful when we want to express our opinion, make a claim about something, or assert an idea.

Noun + な
Casual-form-verb
い-adjective
な-adjective + な

} + のではないだろうか
or
+ のではないかと思う

1. 締め切りまでにこの宿題を終わらせるのは<u>無理</u>なのではないだろうか。
   I would say that finishing this homework before the deadline is impossible.

2. 私のランチを食べたのは<u>彼女</u>ではないのかと思う。
   I suspect that she was the one that ate my lunch.

3. 今年のワールドカップは日本が<u>勝つ</u>のではないかと思う。
   I have a feeling (I think) that Japan is going to win this year's World Cup.

4. 出来るだけ早くこの株を買った方がいいよ。

   おそらくもうすぐ<u>上がる</u>のではないだろうか。
   You should buy this stock as soon as you can. It's likely to go up any time now.

5. 自転車で転んだ男の子はおそらく<u>大丈夫</u>なのではないだろうか。
   The kid that fell off of his bike is probably fine.

6. 道が混んでいるから、東京行きの電車に<u>間</u>に合わないのではないかと思う。
   Because the roads are packed (with other cars), I don't think I'm going to make my train to Tokyo.

7. 日本語よりも中国語の方が<u>簡単なのではないだろうか</u>。

I would say that Chinese is easier than Japanese.

8. 犯人は<u>彼なのではないかと思う</u>。プラム博士はいつも悪いことをするから。

I say that he is the criminal. Professor Plum is always up to no good (always does bad things).

9. 田中は泣いてないと言ったが、本当は<u>泣いていたのではないだろうか</u>。

Tanaka said that he wasn't crying, but I think that he really was.

10. 行ったことはないが、ラスベガスは<u>楽しいのではないかと思う</u>。

いつか行けるといいな…。

I've never been, but Las Vegas has got to be a fun place. I hope I can go some day.

You may be wondering, "What is the difference between the two expressions?" Well, don't worry too much about it because they are the same. In fact, 「のではないだろうか」 and 「のではないかと思う」 are interchangeable. You can substitute one for the other in any of the above sentences, and the meaning would be same.

Another thing you may be wondering is "What is the difference between these structures and 「だろう」 or 「だろうか」?" The answer to that is the "level of certainty."

When we use 「だろう」, we are expressing that whatever we are saying is most likely (almost definitely) true. When we use 「のではないだろうか」 or 「のではないかと思う」 we are fairly confident in what we are saying, but it does not express the same level of confidence as 「だろう」 does. 「だろうか」 would be the least certain of the three. It expresses that whatever we are saying is simply a guess, at best.

11. 今日、彼は来ない<u>だろう</u>。

He is (in all likelihood) not coming today.

12. 今日、彼は来ない<u>のではないかと思う</u>。

I would bet that he is not coming today.

13. 今日、彼は来ないの<u>だろうか</u>。

I wonder if he isn't coming today.

単語を並び替えて、1つの文にしなさい。
Unscramble the following words to make sentences.

(1) I feel that it is going to rain a lot this summer.

多くなる　は　のではないかと思う　の　今年　夏　雨　が

_____。

(2) I bet that worker/employee over there is Mari's little sister.

真理さん　は　あの　スタッフ　なのではないだろうか　の　妹

_____。

(3) If you just keep buying lottery tickets, you'll eventually win some day.

だろう　買い　続けていれば　ずっと　を　当たる　宝くじ　いつかは

_____。

(4) From children's perspective, I feel like this chair is pretty high.

高い　は　この椅子　にとって　のではないだろうか　子供　は

_____。

(5) I feel like this feature may just get in the way (cause problems).

のではないかと思う　邪魔　この　機能　は　な

_____。

(6) I wonder if he is planning on never getting married.

一生　は　つもり　しない　彼　だろうか　結婚

_____。

(7) I wonder what time today's nomikai (drinking party) starts.

から　は　何時　今日　の　飲み会　だろうか

_____？

44

Chapter 11
「〜ておく / 〜でおく」
To be sure to 〜

This next structure is used to express that the listener "do something in advance." It is a little bit difficult to translate into English, but a common translation would be "Be sure to..." or "Make sure to..."

> **て-form-verb + おく**

1. パスポートをスーツケースに<u>入れておく</u>。
   To be sure to put the passport in the suitcase.

2. 鍵をテーブルの上に<u>置いておく</u>。
   To be sure to put the key on the table.

3. 薬を<u>飲んでおく</u>。
   To make sure to take one's medicine.

4. 鍵を<u>閉めておく</u>。
   To be sure to lock the door.

5. 電気を<u>消しておく</u>。
   To be sure to turn off the lights.

Please note that when a verb's て-form ends in 「で」 we say 「でおく」. Like in example sentence 3, 「読む」 becomes 「読んでおく」.

Of course, these sentences aren't very exciting. We can make things a little more interesting by conjugating 「おく」 like any Type I verb. That is to say, we can make it negative, causative, conditional, imperative (a command), etc... the same way we can *any* Type I verb. Here are the above sentences (and some more) with a little more grammatical flair.

6. パスポートをスーツケースに入れておいてください。
   Please be sure to put your passport in your suitcase.

7. 鍵をテーブルの上に置いておいた。
   I made sure to put my keys on the table.

8. 薬を飲まないでおいて。
   Make sure not to take your medicine.

9. 鍵を閉めておきましたか？
   Did you make sure to lock the door?

10. 電気を消しておきなさい。
    Be sure to turn off the light.

11. 日本に来る前に、日本語を勉強しておいて良かった。
    Before coming to Japan, I am glad I made sure to study Japanese.

12. 来週の月曜日までに、このレポートを書いておかないといけない。
    I have to be sure to finish this report by next Monday.

13. ジムに行く前にりんごを食べておこうかな。
    Before going to the gym, I guess I will have an apple.

14. 海外に行くかどうかはまだ決めてないです。考えておきます。
    I haven't decided if I will go abroad or not. I will think about it.

15. 窓を閉めないでおいてください。
    Please be sure to not shut the window.

16. 食べたいだけ食べておけばいい。
    You should just eat however much you want.

It is also worth noting that there is a more casual way to express 「〜ておく」 and 「〜でおく」, and that is to simply shorten them to 「〜とく」 and 「〜どく」, respectively. We are essentially combining the 「て」 and the 「お」 in 「ておく」 to get 「と」, resulting in 「とく」. It is not really hard to imagine how this came about. If you say 「ておく」 or 「〜でおく」fast enough, they will naturally sound like 「とく」 and 「どく」 , so this little phonetic change stuck in conversational Japanese.

Here are what some of the sentences above would look like with this more casual form.

---

17. パスポートをスーツケースに入れといてください。
   Please be sure to put your passport in your suitcase.

18. 鍵をテーブルの上に置いておいてね。
   Make sure to put the keys on the table.

19. 薬を飲んどかないで。
   Make sure not to take your medicine.

20. 鍵を閉めときましたか？
   Did you make sure to lock the door?

21. 電気を消しときなさい。
   Be sure to turn off the lights.

As you can see, the meaning doesn't change. This is just a more casual and natural way of speaking. Of course, this should only be used in casual situations. In formal situations, like when talking with a superior or in business writing, we should always use 「〜ておく」.

擬音語 Japanese Onomatopoeia – "Pain 1"

【じんじん】 Pain that originates from inside the body
Ex. ずっと正座をしていたら、足がじんじんしてきた。
   After sitting in the seiza position for so long, my legs started throbbing in pain.

【ちくちく】 The kind of pain that feels as if you were being pricked by thousands of tiny needles.
Ex. このセーターはちくちくする。
   This sweater prickles my skin.

【きりきり】 A sharp, stabbing pain
Ex. ストレスで胃がきりきりする。
   I experience stomach pains due to stress.

→Answer: P235

最も適切なものを1つ選びなさい。

Choose the right "ておく-phrase" to fill in the blanks.

(1) I gotta buy eggs on my way home from work.

仕事帰りに卵を買っ(   )。

   a. ておきなさい   b. ておきましたか   c. ておかないと   d. ておかないで

(2) Please be sure to bring your *hanko*, just in case.

念のため、はんこを持ってき(   )ください。

   a. ておいて   b. ておかないで   c. ておく   d. ておかないと

(3) Have you been abstaining from alcohol for a while?

しばらく、お酒を飲まない(   )？

   a. でおきますか   b. でおかないと   c. でおいてください   d. でおきましたか

(4) Let's not talk to her about this. She loves gossip.

この話は、彼女には話さない(   )。彼女はおしゃべりだから。

   a. でおかないと   b. でおこう   c. でおかない   d. ておく

(5) Please wait there for a moment.

しばらくそこで待っ(   )ください。

   a. ておいて   b. ておき   c. ておかないで   d. ておく

(6) Good thing I made sure to bring a jacket. This evening suddenly got quite cold.

ジャケットを持ってき(   )よかった。夕方から急に寒くなった。

   a. ておこう   b. ておかないで   c. ておいて   d. ておけば

(7) Did you make sure to take notes so that you don't forget?

忘れないようにしっかりとメモを取っ(   )？

   a. でおく   b. ておきましたか   c. ておく   d. ておかないで

(8) Shall I hand in that report for you (in your stead)?

代わりにそのレポートを提出し(   )？

   a. ておいて   b. ておかないで   c. ておこうか   d. ておきます

Chapter 12
「～くらいなら / ～ぐらいなら」
Would rather ～

We saw earlier how we can use 「くらい」 and 「ぐらい」 to give an estimation, or describe something as being insignificant/inconsequential. In this lesson, we will look at using くらいなら / ぐらいなら to express one alternative being better than another.

Dictionary-form-verb + くらいなら / ぐらいなら

1. 途中で止めるぐらいなら、始めからしない方がいいと思う。
   Instead of quitting half-way through, it would be better to not even start.

2. あの野郎に謝るくらいなら、死んだ方がましだ。
   I'd rather die than apologize to that jerk.

3. ゲームが難しくて泣くぐらいなら、止めた方がいい。
   If the game is so difficult that you'd cry, it would be better to stop (playing it).

4. 嫌な仕事をするくらいなら、貧しくてもいい。
   I'd rather be poor than work a job I didn't like.

Just like before it doesn't matter whether you use くらい or ぐらい. It basically amounts to preference. Use whichever version you feel sounds best or is just easier for you to say.

PRACTICE!

→Answer: P235

（　　　　　）内の単語を使って、1つの文を作りなさい。

Translate the following sentences into Japanese, using 「～くらいなら/～ぐらいなら」.

(1) I would rather just be naked than wear those weird clothes.
（変な服 / 着る / 裸）

_____。

(2) You should just do it instead of regret not having done it.
（後悔 / やる）

_____。

(3) If I have to stand in line, I'd rather not ride the roller coaster.
（並ぶ / ジェットコースター / 乗る）

_____。

(4) Instead of riding train full of people, I'll take a taxi.
（満員電車 / タクシー / 乗る）

_____。

(5) I would prefer to eat natto over umeboshi.
（梅干し / 納豆 / まし）

_____。

Chapter 13

<ruby>違<rt>ちが</rt></ruby>

「～に違いない」
There is no mistaking that ～

This structure is used to express that something is certain or definite, or that we are extremely confident that what we are saying is true. It can be translated as "I am sure" or "there is no doubt that..."

The structure is quite flexible, and can be used with nouns, verbs, and adjectives as is.

> **Noun**
> **Verb**
> **い-adjective**
> **な-adjective**
>
> 　＋ に違いない

Let's look at some example sentences to help illustrate.

1. 俺のランチを食べたのは田中に違いない。
   他の誰かがそんなことをするはずがない。
   It was definitely Tanaka that ate my lunch.
   There's nobody else that would do such a thing.

2. 優秀な山田さんのことだから、時間通りに論文を書き終わるに違いない。
   We are talking about the great Mr. Yamada. He will definitely finish writing his thesis on time.

3. 一人で全部のパーティーの準備をするのは大変に違いない。手を貸そうか？
   Preparing the party all by yourself must be quite stressful/hard. Can I give you a hand?

4. 彼の車は高かったに違いない。いくらだったかな…。
   His car was definitely expensive. I wonder how much it was…

5. トムはこのバーのオーナーと喧嘩したから、もう二度と来ないに違いない。
   Because Tom got in a fight with the owner of this bar, he definitely won't come here again.

If you are familiar with the verb 違う, remembering this structure should be quite easy. 違う means "to be wrong." So, with this grammar structure, what we are essentially saying is "it can't be wrong that..." A more literal translation of example sentence 4 from above would be "It can't be wrong that his car was expensive." Of course, this is not a very natural way to speak English. But, this may help you remember the meaning.

PRACTICE!

→Answer: P235

（　　　　）内の単語を使って、1つの文を作りなさい。

Translate the following sentences into Japanese, using 「〜に違いない」.

(1) That is definitely the sound of a *koto*. （音色 / 琴）

_____。

(2) There is no doubt that she just started learning calligraphy. （書道 / 習い始める）

_____。

(3) The bullet train is definitely fast. （新幹線 / 速い）

_____。

(4) This part-time job will definitely be easy (not demanding mentally or physically).
（アルバイト / 楽）

_____。

(5) That dog is definitely the one that barked just now. （吠える / 犬）

_____。

(6) Even if you go see a Kabuki show, there is no way you'll understand what they're saying.
（歌舞伎 / 観る / 分からない）

_____。

(7) One can be certain that the staff at the information desk are all kind.
（案内係り / スタッフ / 親切）

_____。

Chapter 14

「〜に決まっている」

It must be the case that 〜

Next we have an expression that is quite similar to what we just learned with 〜に違いない. In fact, their meanings are essentially the same. The structure is the exact same, as well. So, if you can use 〜に違いない, this lesson should pose no problem whatsoever. We'll look at a few example sentences, of course, to help illustrate.

```
Noun
Verb          ⎫
い-adjective   ⎬  + に決まっている
な-adjective   ⎭
```

1. 彼のチームは強いから、勝つに決まっています。
   His team is good (strong). They'll definitely win.

2. 彼女は中国人だよ。中国語は話せるに決まっているでしょう。
   She is Chinese, man. Of course, she can speak Chinese.

3. そんなことは無理に決まっているよ。
   That (kind of thing) is, without a doubt, impossible.

4. ボーイフレンドと結婚するって？両親に絶対に反対されるに決まっている。
   You say you're getting married with your boyfriend?
   Your parents will definitely disapprove.

5. あの選手は子供の頃からずっと練習してきたから、すごいに決まっている。
   That player has been playing since he was a child, he is definitely good/tough.

6. 一人でやるなんて、無理に決まっている。助けてください！
   There is no way I can do it by myself. Please help me!

7. 彼が私の自転車を盗んだに決まっている。どうすればいいんだろう。
   He was definitely the one that stole my bike. What should I do?

（　　　　　）内の単語を使って、1つの文を作りなさい。

Translate the following sentences into Japanese, using 「〜に決まっている」.

(1) Of course, onigiri is delicious.

（おにぎり / 美味しい）

_____。

(2) It goes without saying that this brand's products will last a long time.

（メーカー / 製品 / 長持ち）

_____。

(3) There is not questioning the fact that the Grand Canyon is absolutely magnificent.

（グランドキャニオン / 壮大）

_____。

(4) Given the season, it must be a bit chilly outside.

（季節 / 外 / 肌寒い）

_____。

(5) This plan is absolutely absurd.

（計画 / 無茶）

_____。

Chapter 15
「～よう」

In this section, we are going to take a crash course on various uses of 「よう」, of which there are many. I will introduce one structure at a time and break each one down.

I. 「～ようになっている」 Does ～ by itself

First, we'll look at ～ようになっている.

We use ～ようになっている to describe a machine or mechnical device of some kind (a vending machine, a lock, a computer) having some automatic function. This may sound a bit confusing/strange, but if we look at some example sentences, I think it will be clear.

> **Dictionary-form-verbs**
> **ない-form verbs**] + ようになっている

1. 部屋に入ったら、自動的に電気が<u>つくようになっている</u>。
   When you enter the room, the lights automatically come on.

2. このボタンを押すと、お金が<u>出るようになっている</u>。
   When you press this button, the money comes out.

3. このパソコンはパスワードを入力しないと、開くことが<u>できないようになっている</u>。
   If you don't enter the password, you can't open (use) the computer.

4. このドアが閉まると、鍵が<u>かかるようになっている</u>。気を付けて。
   When you close this door, it locks by itself (automatically locks), so be careful.

5. パソコンの電源を切ると、音が<u>出るようになっている</u>。
   The computer makes a sound (by itself) when you turn it off.

II. 「～ような / ～ように」
Giving ～ as an example; Exactly ～; Describing your goals

Next, we'll look at using ～ような and ～ように.

We use ～ような and ～ように when we want to give something as an example. We can use it to describe the way something looks or how something is done. These two structures function very similarly to "like." We use 「ような」 when describing a noun and 「ように」 when describing a verb.

| Noun Verb | + ような / ように |

1. 赤やオレンジのような明るい色がすごく好き。
   I really like bright colors like red and orange.

2. メンちゃんのように中国語を話せるようになりたいな。
   I want to be able to speak Chinese like Men-chan does.

3. 彼女のようにきれいになりたい。
   I want to be pretty like her.

4. 彼が履いているような靴が欲しい。どこで買ったのだろう。
   I want shoes like the ones he has. I wonder where he bought them.

5. あなたのように練習したら、僕もバスケが上手になるね。
   If I practice like you, I'll get good at basketball too, eh.

We can see in sentence 1 that because we are giving examples of bright colors that we like (red and orange), that we need to use 「ような」 (since colors are nouns). Likewise, in sentence 2, we are giving the way Men-chan speaks Chinese as an example of how we would also like to speak Chinese. And since "speak" is a verb, we need to use 「ように」.

Now we'll look at another way of using ～ように for a different purpose.

～ように can also be used with nouns and verbs to describe something as being "exactly that way." Some example sentences will help make it clear.

| Noun Verb | + ように |

6. 上司に言われたように仕事をやったけど、また怒られた。

I did exactly what the boss told me, but he still got mad at me.

7. 子供が親の思うようにならないのは当たり前でしょう。

It's only natural that children don't turn out exactly the way parents hope they will.

8. あなたは先生が言うように全部やったら、絶対にＪＬＰＴに合格するよ。

If you do everything (the way) the teacher says, you'll definitely pass the JLPT.

9. 本に書いてあるようにしているけど、全然うまくいかない。

I am doing it exactly how it is written in the book, but it is not going well at all.

～ように also has another use, and that is to describe something as being one's goal, objective, or aim.

> **Verb's potential-form + ない-form + ように**

10. 眠くならないように、クラスに来る前にコーヒーを飲んでおいた。

So that I don't get sleepy in class, I make sure to drink a cup of coffee before coming.

11. 遅刻しないように、早く家を出るつもりです。

In order to not be late, I am planning on leaving the house early.

12. 英語を忘れないように、毎週英語の新聞を読むことにしている。

To help make sure that I don't forget English, I read an English newspaper every week.

13. 太らないように、週3回ジムに通っています。

I go to the gym three times a week so that I do not gain weight.

We have to be careful, however, because this structure is often confused with「ために」, which is also used to express something as being a goal or objective. The difference is, we use「ために」in conjunction with activities we do with a conscious effort. For example...

Ex. 日本語を勉強するために日本に来ることにした。

I came to Japan for the purpose of studying Japanese.

We can see this differs from example sentence 12 from above, in that whether we "forget English" or not isn't a decision we can make ourselves. There are things we can do to prevent it from happening, but we cannot consciously force ourselves to forget or not forget.

III. 「～ようがない」 No way to ～

Now we'll take a look at our final ～よう structure of this textbook, and that is ～ようがない.

We use ～ようがない to describe something as being out of our control or impossible to do. Another common translation is "there is no way to [verb]."

> **Verb's ます-stem + ようがない**

1. 私は<u>救いようがない</u>馬鹿なんだ！
   I am an idiot who is beyond saving! (I am a complete and under moron!)

2. 彼は私の言うことを全く聞かない。やっぱり、彼は<u>助けようがない</u>。
   He won't listen to what I say at all. Like I said, there is no way to help him.

3. 彼女の携帯番号をなくしてしまったから、彼女に<u>連絡しようがない</u>。
   I lost her cell phone number, so I have no way to contact her.

4. 僕は英語ができないから、アメリカ人と<u>会話しようがない</u>。
   I can't speak English, so I have no way to converse with Americans.

5. その本の漢字は難しすぎる。私には<u>読みようがない</u>。
   That book's Kanji is too difficult. There is no way I can read it.

If we look at sentence 1, we can see that the verb is 救う (to save/rescue) and that the ます-form is 救います. All we do is drop ます and append ようがない to get 救いようがない, which basically translates to "there is no way to save."

擬音語 Japanese Onomatopoeia – "Pain 2"

【しくしく】 A dull, constant pain; not very strong
Ex. お腹が<u>しくしく</u>痛む。
I have a dull, constant stomachache.

【ずきずき】 Pain that comes on like a wave.
Ex. 頭が<u>ずきずき</u>する。
My head is throbbing with pain.

【がんがん】 A pounding headache.
Ex. 二日酔いで頭が<u>がんがん</u>する。
This hangover is giving me a splitting headache.

 **PRACTICE!**

→Answer: P235

最も適切なものを1つ選びなさい。
Choose the right phrase to fill in the blanks.

(1) You can now view your grades on the Internet.
　　成績はインターネットで（　　　　　）。

　　a. 閲覧するようになっている　　b. 閲覧しようがない　　c. 閲覧しないように

(2) Those two suit each other perfectly.
　　彼らは双子の（　　　　　）息がぴったりだね。

　　a. ような　　b. ようがない　　c. ように　　d. ようになっている

(3) It feels as if I am at the center of mother nature.
　　まるで大自然の中にいる（　　　　　）感じがする。

　　a. ように　　b. ようになっている　　c. ようがない　　d. ような

(4) There is no way I could mix up her birthday because it is the same as mine.
　　彼女の誕生日を間違え（　　　　　）。僕と同じ誕生日だから。

　　a. ように　　b. ような　　c. ようがない　　d. ないように

(5) Make absolutely sure not to be late for next week's meeting.
　　再来週の会議には絶対に（　　　　　）。

　　a. 遅刻するように　　b. 遅刻しないように　　c. 遅刻しようがない　　d. 遅刻ような

(6) You can't go to the library today. It is closed.
　　今日、図書館に入館（　　　　　）。休館日らしい。

　　a. できるようになっている　　b. できようがない　　c.できないようになっている

(7) Don't believe everything that he says. You should take what he says with a grain of salt.
　　彼の話を全部信じ（　　　　　）ね。話半分で聞いた方がいい。

　　a. ようがない　　b. るようになっている　　c. るように　　d. ないように

(8) I want a clock like the one my brother has.
　　お兄ちゃんが持っている（　　　　　）時計が欲しいな。

　　a. ように　　b. ような　　c. ようがない　　d. ようになっている

Chapter 16
「～わけ」

In this section, we are going to take a look at a number of uses for 「わけ」. There are quite a few, so we'll take a look at them one by one and break them down.

I. 「～わけ」 Giving a reason

The word 「わけ」 by itself simply means "reason" or "situation." The following examples will help illustrate.

1. あなたの誕生日を忘れてしまってごめんなさい。でも、これには<u>わけ</u>があるのです。
   I am sorry I ended up forgetting your birthday, but I have a good reason.

2. 彼女はいつも嘘をつく。まったく<u>わけ</u>が分からないな…。
   She always tells lies. I don't understand her at all…

「わけ」 can also be used as another word for 'meaning.'

3. あの人は<u>わけ</u>の分からないことをずっと話していた。酔っていたかな？
   That guy kept talking complete nonsense. I wonder if her was drunk.

4. 壁に<u>わけ</u>が分からないメッセージが書いてある。君は分かる？
   There is a message that I cannot understand written on the wall. Do you get/understand it?

We can also combine 「わけ」 with 「(が)ない」 to get 「わけ(が)ない」, which means something is easy or didn't pose any kind of problem.

5. 今日の日本語の試験はすごく簡単だったよ。

   ひらがなとカタカナを書くくらいだった。<u>わけがなかった</u>。
   Today's Japanese test was super easy.
   We basically just had to write Hiragana and Katakana. It was a piece of cake.

6. 今日の宿題は全然難しくなかったよ。<u>わけなく</u>できた。手伝ってあげようか？
   Today's homework wasn't difficult in the least. I did it with no trouble at all.
   Shall I help you (with it)?

II. 「〜わけだ」 Pointing out a fact; Explaining the cause of something

We saw before that 「わけ」 is a word by itself that means "reason" or "situation." We can also combine it with verbs and adjectives to point out something obvious, or to draw a logical conclusion. Let's look at a few example sentences.

Verb **な-adjective** **い-adjective**	**+ わけだ**

1. 20歳の時に日本に引っ越した。今、３３歳。
   もう10年以上日本に<u>住んでいるわけだ</u>。
   When I was 20 years old, I moved to Japan. Now I am 33.
   That means I have been living Japan for over 10 years.

2. 父と母はロシア人だけど、彼女はアメリカで生まれた。
   つまり、彼女はアメリカ人で<u>あるわけだ</u>。
   Her dad and mom are Russian, but she was born in America.
   In other words, she is an American.

3. 太陽から一番近い惑星は水星です。
   つまり、太陽系の惑星の中で一番<u>熱いわけだ</u>。
   The closest planet to the sun is Mercury.
   To put it another way, it is the hottest planet in our solar system.

4. 彼は毎日パソコンを使う。目が<u>悪いわけだ</u>。
   He uses a computer every day. Therefore, his eyes are bad.

Another use of 「〜わけだ」 is to understand and then explain the reason or cause of something.

5. インターネットが<u>つながらないわけだ</u>。ここのWi-Fiのパスワードが変わっていた。
   No wonder I can't connect to the Wi-Fi here. The password has changed.

6. 彼は<u>強いわけだ</u>。子供の頃からずっとボクシングをやっているそうだ。
   Of course, he is strong/good. I heard that he has been boxing since he was just a kid.

7. 僕は最近ゲームばかりしている。成績が<u>悪くなるわけだ</u>。
   Lately I've done nothing but play games. That would explain why my grades are getting worse.

8. 今朝、雨が降っていた。道が濡れているわけだ。

It was raining this morning. That would explain why the road is wet.

9. 中国語って、全ての文字が漢字なの？勉強するのが大変なわけだ。

In Chinese, all of the words are Kanji characters? No wonder it is so hard to study.

Another use of 「わけだ」 is to explain the reason for something, and takes on a feeling of "that's why..."

10. 明日生徒たちは早く起きないといけない。それでみんなもう寝ているわけだ。

Tomorrow, the students have to wake up early. That's why they are all already asleep.

11. 彼は卒業してから全然運動してないって。それでちょっと太ってきたわけだ。

He says that he hasn't done any exercise since graduating. That's why he has gained a little weight.

12. もともと1年くらいだけ日本にいるつもりだったが、いい友達ができて、給料がいい仕事も見つけて、日本に住み続けられることになったわけです。

Originally, I only planned on being in Japan for a year, but I made some good friends and found a high-paying job. That is how I came to stay in Japan.

擬音語 Japanese Onomatopoeia – "Cleaning"

【ぴかぴか】 To be glossy or shine brilliantly.
Ex. 車をぴかぴかになるように洗った。
I washed my car until it shined.

【つるつる】 A surface is very smooth
Ex. ワックスを塗ったから、床がつるつるになった。
I waxed the floor, so now it is smooth/shiny.

【ぬるぬる】 Slippery
Ex. ずっと掃除していなかったから、プールの底がぬるぬるしている。
I haven't cleaned the pool in a long time, so the bottom is all slimy.

【ごちゃごちゃ】 Various objects are mixed together and strewn about haphazardly
Ex. 彼の部屋はごちゃごちゃしていて、全然リラックス出来ない。
His room is in such a mess that I can't relax at all.

III. 「〜わけがない」 Can't possibly be 〜

The next 「わけ」 structure we'll look at is used to express that something "couldn't possibly be," or that "of course that isn't true." We can use it with verbs, adjectives, and nouns.

1. 昨日、日本語の勉強を始めたばかりだから、その漢字を<u>読めるわけない</u>だろう。
   I only started studying Japanese yesterday. There is no way I could read that Kanji.

2. パリでこの靴を買ったのですよ。<u>安かったわけがない</u>。
   I bought these shoes in Paris. Of course they weren't cheap!

3. 東京が<u>静かなわけがない</u>でしょう。人が多すぎる。
   There is no way Tokyo is quiet. There are too many people.

4. 彼女は日本語ができません。日本人で<u>あるわけがありません</u>。
   She can't speak Japanese. There is no way she is Japanese.

5. 小さい子供がダンクシュート<u>できるわけない</u>でしょう。
   Of course a child can't dunk (a basketball).

擬音語 (ぎおんご) Japanese Onomatopoeia – "Laughing 1"

【くすくす】 Laughing quietly so as not to be heard by others
Ex. 先生の後ろ髪がはねていたので、生徒達はくすくす笑っていた。
The hair on the back of the teacher's head was messed up, and the students were laughing at her behind her back.

【にこにこ】 Smile happily without making any sound
Ex. あの人はいつも<u>にこにこ</u>していて、幸せそうだね。
That person always has a smile on her face. She seems so happy.

【けらけら】 High-pitched laugh
【けたけた】
Ex. コメディーショーを家族みんなで<u>けらけら</u>笑いながら観た。
While laughing boisterously, the family watched the comedy show.
Ex. 息子が漫画を読みながら、<u>けたけた</u>笑っている。
My son is reading manga and laughing wildly.

IV. 「〜わけではない」 Not necessarily 〜

The next structure we'll look at is used to express that something "isn't necessarily so," though it could be. And that whatever is being said perhaps goes against what one might naturally think.

> **Verb**
> **な-adjective + な**   **+ わけではない**
> **い-adjective**

1. 背が高いからといってバスケが得意なわけではない。
   People that are tall aren't necessarily good at basketball.

2. 背が低いからといってバスケが下手なわけではない。
   People that are short aren't necessarily bad at basketball.

3. それほど高いわけではないが、もっと安いのを買いたいと思う。
   It's not that it's too expensive, but I think I'd rather by one that is a bit cheaper.

4. アメリカ人がみんな英語を教えられるわけではない。簡単な仕事ではないよ。
   Not all Americans can teach English. It's not an easy job.

5. あなたの言いたいことは分からないわけではないが、駄目なことは駄目なんだ。
   It's not that I don't understand what you want to say, but no means no.

擬音語 Japanese Onomatopoeia – "Laughing 2"

【にやにや】   To smile faintly without making any audible sounds
   Ex. サプライズプレゼントを持った子ども達は、にやにやしながらおばあちゃんの家に向かった。
   The children were grinning as they headed over to their grandmother's house to give her a surprise present.

【にたにた】   Smirk or smile grimly without making any sound (while thinking of a bad thing). Most often used in a negative way.
   Ex. その犯人は、戸惑っている警察官を遠くから見てにたにたしていた。
   That criminal looked at the puzzled police officer from afar and was smirking.

64

V. 「～わけにはいかない」 Couldn't possibly ～

The next structure we'll look at is used to describe matters of conscience or societal issues as being unacceptable or simply undoable.

> **Dictionary-form-verb ＋ わけにはいかない**

1. 明日は大事な試験があるから、学校をさぼるわけにはいかないよ。
   I have an important test tomorrow, so there is no way I could skip class.

2. すみません、車で来たのでお酒を飲むわけにはいかないです。
   Sorry, but I drove here. I can't drink any alcohol.

3. 靴を履いたまま家に入るわけにはいかない。
   You must never go into the house with your shoes on.

4. 悪いことをしてしまっても、子供を殴るわけにはいかない。
   Even if your child does something bad, hitting them is inexcusable.

VI. 「～ないわけにはいかない」 ～must be so; Have no choice but to ～

We have finally made it to our last 「わけ」 structure of this textbook. It's a mouthful, but if you're comfortable with the previously taught structures, then this shouldn't pose too much of a problem, as it simply builds off of what we have learned.

This structure basically has the opposite meaning of what we saw with 「～わけにはいかない」. The 「ない」 at the front should help make this clear. And what we are saying with this structure is that based on some reason we *have* to do something, but, in reality, don't want to.

> **Verb's ない-form ＋ わけにはいかない**

1. これは美味しくないけど、彼女が作ってくれたから食べないわけにはいかない。
   This doesn't taste very good, but my girlfriend made it for me so I have to eat it.

2. 上司の冗談はあんまり面白くないけど、笑わないわけにはいかないでしょう。
   The boss's jokes aren't really funny, but I have no choice but to laugh.

3. 来年日本へ留学するから、日本語を身につけないわけにはいかない。
   I am going to study abroad in Japan, so I have to learn Japanese.

65

最も適切なものを1つ選びなさい。
Choose the right phrase to fill in the blanks.

(1) I have a good reason for breaking my promise.
私が約束を破ったのには深い(　　　　)。

    a. わけではない　　b. わけがある　　c. わけにはいかない　　d. わけがあるに違いない

(2) For someone like him who has a bottomless pit for a stomach, he'll have no problem whatsoever eating all of this.
食欲旺盛な彼にとっては、このくらいは(　　　　)食べれる。

    a. わけなく　　b. わけない　　c. わけには　　d.わけがある

(3) I hear that she meditates every morning. No wonder she is always so calm.
彼女は毎朝瞑想をしているらしい。どうりでおおらか(　　　　)。

    a. わけだ　　b. なわけだ　　c. なわけがある　　d. なわけがない

(4) Because I am receiving a scholarship, there're no way that I could slack off on my studies.
奨学金をもらっているからには、勉強(　　　　)。

    a. するわけなかった　　b. するわけがない　　c. しないわけだ　　d. しないわけにはいかない

(5) There is no way that a child who hates Disneyland could exist.
ディズニーランドが嫌いな子供がいる(　　　　)。

    a. わけではない　　b. わけにはいかない　　c. わけがない　　d.わけだ

(6) I cannot understand that professor's theory whatsoever.
あの教授の理論は(　　　　)。

    a.わけなかった　　b. わけが分からない　　c. わけがない　　d.わけがあるに違いない

(7) "I forgot to add salt to the food!" "No wonder the taste is so bland."
「料理に塩を入れ忘れていた！」「どうりで味が物足りない(　　　　)。」

    a. わけだ　　b. わけがある　　c. わけなかった　　d. わけ

(8) Just because it is from a 100-Yen shop doesn't necessarily mean that the quality is poor.
100均の商品だからといって、安っぽい(　　　　)。

    a. わけがない　　b. わけえだ　　c. わけがある　　d. わけではない

Chapter 17
「〜からといって」 Just because 〜

I found myself using this structure quite regularly when I was in Japan. It basically means something like "Just because X, doesn't mean Y." You'll also often see this structure used in conjunction with 「限<ruby>限<rt>かぎ</rt></ruby>らない」, which helps emphasize the perception of an idea versus the reality.

Verb **Noun** + だ **な-adjective** + だ **い-adjective**	+ からといって

1. アメリカ人だからといって、日本語が出来ないとは限らないよ。
   Just because I am American doesn't mean I can't speak Japanese.

2. 背が高いからといって、バスケが好きだとは限らない。
   Just because someone is tall doesn't mean they like basketball.

3. 泣いているからといって、悲しんでいるわけではない。
   Just because someone cries doesn't necessarily mean they are sad.

4. ジムに通っているからといって、絶対に痩せるとは限らないよ。
   ちゃんと運動しないと。
   Just because you are going to the gym doesn't mean you will lose weight, you know.
   You have to actually work out.

5. 女性だからといって、体が弱いとは限らない。
   Just because she is a girl doesn't mean that she is weak.

（　　　　　）内の単語を使って、1つの文を作りなさい。

Translate the following sentences into Japanese, using 「～からといって」.

(1) Just because someone is a lawyer doesn't mean that they know all of the laws.
（弁護士 / 全ての法律）

_____。

(2) Just because someone is fashionable doesn't necessarily mean that they have a lot of clothes. （おしゃれ / 服）

_____。

(3) Just because they are good friends doesn't mean that they are always together.
（仲がいい / 一緒にいる）

_____。

(4) Liking alcohol doesn't necessarily mean that one can drink a lot. （お酒 / 飲む）

_____。

(5) I know you are the shy type, but you still shouldn't be so cold to her.
（照れくさい / 冷たく）

_____。

(6) Just because you are feeling better doesn't mean you should push it by exerting yourself too much. （体調 / 調子に乗る）

_____。

(7) Not using a handbag because it is expensive would be a waste.
（高価な / もったいない）

_____。

Chapter 18
「～てたまらない」
Describing extreme cases

This structure allows us to express that something has reached an extreme level that we can no longer stand or bear.

> て-form of adjective that express a feeling of emotion ＋ たまらない

1. 北海道の冬は寒くてたまらない。もう、アリゾナに帰りたい！
   The winters in Hokkaido are so cold I can't stand it. I just want to go back to Arizona!

2. あの子犬はかわいくてたまらない！写真を撮ろう！
   That puppy is so cute, I can't stand it! Let's take a picture!

3. 学生の頃、歴史のクラスは嫌でたまらなかったけど、今は結構好き。
   When I was a student, I hated history class with a passion. But now, I quite like it (history).

4. 次のワンピースの単行本が読みたくてたまらない！今の話はすごく面白いね！
   I want to read the next One Piece book so bad! The current story is so good, right?!

As we can see in sentence 2, this expression doesn't always have to express a negative feeling. Just like how in English we might say, "The baby is so cute I can't stand it!" Of course, a majority of the time, it is used to express some form of dissatisfaction.

Japanese Onomatopoeia – "Busy"

【ばたばた】   Busy, hurried, hustling and bustling; no time to rest
Ex. 引っ越し前で、ばたばたしています。
I'm moving soon and am busy as a bee.

【せかせか】   Speaking in an irritated, uneasy, or impatient manner
Ex. 彼女はやらなければいけないことがたくさんあるので、一日中せかせかしている。
She has many things that she must do every day, so she speaks in a short, curt tone all day.

→Answer: P236

（　　　　）内の単語を使って、1つの文を作りなさい。

Translate the following sentences into Japanese, using「たまらない」.

(1) I'm so hungry I could eat a horse.

（お腹 / 減る）

_____。

(2) Living by myself is terribly lonely.

（ひとり暮らし / さみしい）

_____。

(3) My pet cat is absolutely adorable.

（ペット / 愛しい）

_____。

(4) I used to feel completely hopeless, but I gradually got used to it.

（心細い / だんだん / 慣れ）

_____。

(5) At first I thought this book was completely stupid, but it gradually became more and more interesting.

（ばかばかしい / 徐々に / 面白い）

_____。

Chapter 19
「〜から〜にかけて」 From 〜 to ...

This next expression is used to describe the distance between two physical objects, or two points in time.

Noun + から + Noun + にかけて

1. 4月から１１月にかけてアリゾナは暑いよ。
   From April to November it is hot in Arizona.

2. 春は北海道から九州にかけてどこに行っても桜が見られる。
   In spring you can see cherry blossoms from Hokkaido down to Kyushu.

3. 天田さんは頭から足にかけてタトゥーを入れている。
   Mr. Amada is covered in tattoos from head to toe.

4. 昨晩から今朝にかけてずっと雨が降っていた。
   From last night until this morning it rained and rained.

擬音語（ぎおんご） **Japanese Onomatopoeia – "Eating 1"**

【あつあつ】　Food is hot (temperature-wise)
　　　　　　Ex. あつあつのすき焼きを食べたら、体が温まった。
　　　　　　　　When I ate the hot sukiyaki, my body warmed up.

【ほくほく】　Something that has been roasted (chestnuts, sweet potatoes, etc...) and is now soft and warm
　　　　　　Ex. このスイートポテトは、ほくほくして美味しい。
　　　　　　　　This sweet potato is so soft and warm. It's delicious.

【もちもち】　Slightly springy; somewhat elastic
　　　　　　Ex. 大福は、もちもちのお餅の中にあんこが入っている食べ物です。
　　　　　　　　Daifuku is a kind of mochi that has anko inside.

→Answer: P236

「〜から〜にかけて」を使って、2つの文を1つの文にしなさい。

Take the following sentences and combine them into one, using 「-から-にかけて」.

(1) Class started at 10:00. Then, it was over at 12:00.

授業は10時に始まった。そして、12時に終わった。

_____。

(2) The traffic congestion starts at the residential district and goes all the way to the station.

渋滞は住宅地から始まっている。そして、駅前まで続いている。

_____。

(3) I took off from Nagoya by car and arrived in Tokyo.

車で名古屋を出発した。そして、東京に着いた。

_____。

72

Chapter 20
「～おかげで」 Thanks to ～

We can use 「おかげで」 to give the reason for something. It is typically used with positive results, and can be translated as "thanks to ～" It can be used with nouns, verbs, and adjectives. But with nouns, we need to include 「の」.

Verb Noun + の な-adjective い-adjective	+ おかげで

1. さやか先生のおかげで日本語を話せるようになりました。
   Because of Miss Sayaka, I learned to speak Japanese.

2. 明子さんが助けてくれたおかげで、早く今日の宿題がすみました。
   Thanks to the help I got from Miss Akiko, I was able to finish my homework quicker than usual.

3. 尾田先生のおかげで、日本の文化に興味を持ちました。
   Thanks to Mr. Oda, I become interested in Japanese culture.

4. ボブのおかげで仕事に遅刻してしまった。
   Thanks to Bob, I was late for work.

5. コーヒーのおかげで最後まで彼の講義を聴けました。
   Thanks to my coffee, I was able to listen to his lecture to the very end.

We can see here in example sentence 4 that 「～おかげで」 can be used for negative results, as well, when used in an obviously sarcastic way, but for a vast majority of the time, it will be used to express something positive.

→Answer: P236

（　　　　）内の単語を使って、1つの文を作りなさい。

Translate the following sentences into Japanese, using 「おかげで」.

(1) I can now read manga thanks to the effort I put into learning Japanese.
（勉強 / 漫画）

_____ 。

(2) Thanks to everyone, my life as an international student was fun.
（みなさん / 留学生活）

_____ 。

(3) Due to my job being so easy, over time, I became lazy.
（どんどん / 怠け者）

_____ 。

(4) Thanks to my alarm clock, I was able to wake up on time.
（目覚まし時計 / ちゃんと）

_____ 。

(5) Because of the great service and attention paid to details, my stay at the ryokan was very relaxing.
（旅館 / きめ細かい）

_____ 。

Chapter 21
「〜っけ」 What was that again...?

This structure looks rather odd at first, but if you have any experience speaking Japanese casually with friends, then there is no doubt that you have heard this used hundreds (if not thousands) of times. I say "casually with friends" because this is a rather casual expression and won't typically be seen in writing, or used in the office.

It is basically used as a way to check or confirm something from the past as being true. I realize that may sound a little complicated, but it is quite simple. And because it is checking something from the past, we almost always need to use it with the past-tense form of a noun, adjective, or verb. Though, there is an exception with the copula 「です」 that we will see in the example sentences below.

> **Verb**
> **Past-tense-form of noun**
> **な-adjective**
> **い-adjective**　　　　＋ っけ

1. あれ、私、さっき携帯をどこに<u>置いたっけ</u>？
   Huh, where did I put my phone just now?

2. 明日のミーティングは<u>いつだったっけ（いつだっけ）</u>？
   When is tomorrow's meeting again?

3. えっ、私がそんなことを本当に<u>言ったっけ</u>？
   Huh, did I really say something like that?

4. 来週の出張は<u>どこだったっけ（どこだっけ）</u>？
   Where was next week's business trip again?

5. パーティーには何人<u>来るんだったっけ</u>…？
   How many people are coming to the party again...?
   (How many people was it that are coming?)

6. 彼はいつ来るって<u>言ったっけ</u>？
   What day did he say he was coming again?
   (What day was it that he said he was coming?)

We can see from example sentences 2 and 4 that we can shorten 「だったっけ」 to just 「だっけ」. The meaning is exactly the same, and whichever one you wish to use is simply a matter of preference.

I think example sentence 5 is rather instructional as well. Here, we are using 「です」 right after the dictionary-form-verb 「来る」. Without using 「っけ」 this sentence would likely just be...

Ex. パーティーには何人来ますか？

How many people are coming to the party?

We don't want to ask, 「パーティーに何人来たっけ？」 because that would be "How many people was it that came to the party again...?" and the party the people are coming to hasn't been held yet. So, the party the speaker is asking about in example sentence 5 is actually set to happen in the future. But, how many people are supposed to come has already been determined, and the speaker is trying to remember what that number was. That is why 「来る」 is in the non-past-tense form, while the copula is in the past-tense.

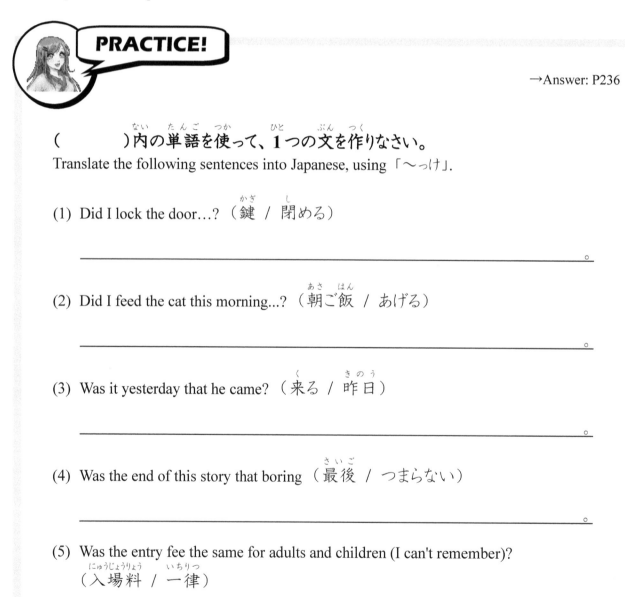

PRACTICE!

→Answer: P236

（　　　　　）内の単語を使って、1つの文を作りなさい。

Translate the following sentences into Japanese, using 「〜っけ」.

(1) Did I lock the door...? （鍵 / 閉める）

_____ 。

(2) Did I feed the cat this morning...? （朝ご飯 / あげる）

_____ 。

(3) Was it yesterday that he came? （来る / 昨日）

_____ 。

(4) Was the end of this story that boring （最後 / つまらない）

_____ 。

(5) Was the entry fee the same for adults and children (I can't remember)?
（入場料 / 一律）

_____ 。

Chapter 22
「～ちゃ/じゃ」 & 「～ちゃう/じゃう」
Speaking more colloquially

Since the last structure we looked at with 「っけ」 was a casual, spoken structure, I thought we'd follow it up with some other casual, spoken structures. This isn't a grammar lesson, as you should already be familiar with the 「～て/ではいけません」 and 「～て/でしまう」 structures. It is more of a lesson in "how to speak more casually."

If you are familiar with how to use 「～て/ではいけません」 and 「～て/でしまう」 then this will be really easy to learn. If you are not familiar with these grammar structures, however, I suggest you review them (perhaps by using my first book) before studying this little lesson.

First we'll look at 「～て/ではいけません」.

In spoken Japanese, it is common for people to change the 「ては」 of 「～てはいけません」 to 「ちゃ」 and the 「では」 of 「ではいけません」 to 「じゃ」

> ～ては → ～ちゃ
> ～では → ～じゃ

1. タバコを<u>吸って</u>はいけません。　→　タバコを<u>吸っちゃ</u>いけません。
   You mustn't smoke.

2. お酒を<u>飲んで</u>はいけない。　→　お酒を<u>飲んじゃ</u>いけない。
   Don't drink (alcohol).

3. 大声で<u>話して</u>はだめ。　→　大声で<u>話しちゃ</u>だめ。
   No speaking in a loud voice.

4. 漫画を<u>読んで</u>はだめ。　→　漫画を<u>読んじゃ</u>だめ。
   You mustn't read manga.

Similarly, the 「て」 of 「てしまう」 will be spoken as 「ちゃう」 and the 「で」 of 「でしまう」 will be spoken as 「じゃう」 in casual Japanese.

$$
\begin{aligned}
&〜てしまう \quad → \quad 〜ちゃう\\
&〜でしまう \quad → \quad 〜じゃう
\end{aligned}
$$

5. 宿題を忘れてしまった。　→　宿題を忘れちゃった。
   I forgot my homework (oh no!)

6. 全部使ってしまう。　→　全部使っちゃう。
   To use up every thing.

7. 1日で読んでしまう。　→　1日で読んじゃう。
   To finish reading in a single day.

8. 一人で飲んでしまった。　→　一人で飲んじゃった。
   I ended up drinking all of it by myself.

擬音語 Japanese Onomatopoeia – "Eating 2"

【しゃきしゃき】　Something is fresh and crunchy
Ex. このレタスはしゃきしゃきで美味しいね。
This lettuce has a nice crunch and is quite good.

【ずるずる】　Slurping sound made when eating noodles
Ex. ラーメンをずるずると食べる。
Eat ramen while making slurping sounds.

【ふわふわ】　Extremely soft
Ex. ふわふわのパンケーキの作り方を知っている？
Do you know how to make light, fluffy pancakes?

【とろとろ】　Something hard that has become soft
Ex. チーズフォンデュは、とろとろのチーズに好きな食べ物をからめて食べる料理です。
Cheese fondue is a dish that is eaten by dipping a food you like into melted cheese.

【ねばねば】　Sticky
Ex. 納豆はねばねばしているから、嫌い。
I don't like natto because it is so sticky

【ぷりぷり】　Something is tight and springy
Ex. この新鮮なエビはぷりぷりしているね。
This shrimp is fresh and plump.

（　　　　　）に「ちゃ」、「じゃ」、「ちゃう/ちゃった」、「じゃう/じゃった」のいずれかを入れなさい。

Fill in the (　)'s with either「ちゃ」,「じゃ」,「ちゃう/ちゃった」 or 「じゃう/じゃった」.

(1) No talking on the phone while riding public transportation.

公共交通機関の中で電話をし（　　　　　　　　　）いけません。

(2) Whenever I swim in a pool, I always end up swallowing the water.

プールで泳ぐ時、どうしてもプールの水を飲ん（　　　　　　　　）。

(3) People under 20 are prohibited from drinking.

二十歳未満の人は、お酒を飲ん（　　　　　　　　）いけません。

(4) Against my better judgment, I always end up eating too much candy.

ついつい、いつもお菓子を食べ過ぎ（　　　　　　）。

(5) I ended up doing it again...

またやっ（　　　　　　　　）。

(6) You mustn't run on the station platform.

駅のホームでは走っ（　　　　　　　）だめですよ。

(7) It's hot, so I took of my jacket.

暑いから、ジャケットを脱い（　　　　　　　）。

(8) Don't bite your nails.

指の爪を嚙ん（　　　　　　）だめ。

Chapter 23
「〜について」&
「〜に関する / 〜に関し（て）」

I. 「〜について」 About 〜

Here we have a nice little grammar structure that can be used on a daily basis and is definitely one you'll want to practice. We can use 「〜について」 with nouns to identify them as the topic of a sentence, and translates roughly to "about ~" or "regarding ~"

Noun + について

1. この事件について何か分かりますか？
   Do you know anything about this incident?

2. 来週のテストについて話したくない。全然準備が出来ていない。
   I don't want to talk about next week's test. I am not ready for it at all.

3. 日本の歴史について勉強したいと思ったから来日しました。
   I wanted to learn about Japanese history, so I decided to come to Japan.

4. この映画についての意見を教えてください。
   Please tell me your opinion about this movie.

擬音語 **Japanese Onomatopoeia – "Eating 3"**

【くちゃくちゃ】 To make noise while eating with your mouth open
Ex. くちゃくちゃと食べてはいけません。
Don't eat with your mouth open.

【もぐもぐ】 To eat without opening your mouth wide.
Ex. 子供達は、クッキーをもぐもぐ食べながらテレビを観ている。
The children are munching on cookies while watching television.

II. 「～に関(かん)する / ～に関(かん)し(て)」 Regarding ～

This structure is very similar to what we saw with 「～について」 and, in fact, has the exact same meaning. It also has the use of showing the relationship of something, and can be translated as "in relation to" or "related to."

$$\text{Noun} + \left[\begin{array}{l} \text{に関(かん)する} \\ \text{に関(かん)し(て)} \end{array} \right.$$

5. 中国(ちゅうごく)の歴史(れきし)に関(かん)する本(ほん)を買(か)いたいと思(おも)います。
   I want to buy a book about (dealing with) Chinese history.

6. アメリカに留学(りゅうがく)することに関(かん)し(おし)て教えてください。
   Please tell me about (anything related to) studying abroad in America.

7. 彼女(かのじょ)は数学(すうがく)だけでなく、科学(かがく)に関(かん)しても結構(けっこう)詳(くわ)しいよ。
   質問(しつもん)があったら、彼女(かのじょ)に聞(き)いた方(ほう)がいい。
   She is not only knowledgeable about math, but chemistry as well.
   If you have a question, you should ask her.

8. すみません、経済(けいざい)に関(かん)する教科書(きょうかしょ)はどこですか？
   Excuse me, where are your books on (related to) economics?

9. 僕(ぼく)の両親(りょうしん)はパソコンに関(かん)してあまり詳(くわ)しくない。メールくらいしかできない。
   Neither of my parents is particularly familiar with computers.
   Just about the only thing they can do is e-mail.

擬音語(ぎおんご)

Japanese Onomatopoeia – "Eating 4"

【ごくごく】　To gulp down
Ex. 喉(のど)が渇(かわ)いていたので、ごくごくと水(みず)を飲(の)んだ。
I was thirsty, so I chugged a glass of water.

【きんきん】　Something is chilled and very cold
Ex. 暑(あつ)いときは、きんきんのビールがとても美味(おい)しい。
When it's hot, ice-cold beer is so good.

（　　　　　）内の単語を使って、1つの文を作りなさい。

Translate the following sentences into Japanese.

(1) I don't know anything about this.

（このこと /に関して / 知る）

＿＿＿＿＿＿＿＿＿＿＿＿＿＿＿＿＿＿＿＿＿＿＿＿＿＿＿＿＿＿。

(2) Her knowledge regarding penguins is vast.

（ペンギン /に関する / 豊富）

＿＿＿＿＿＿＿＿＿＿＿＿＿＿＿＿＿＿＿＿＿＿＿＿＿＿＿＿＿＿。

(3) At this meeting, we are going to discuss environmental protection.

（会議 /について / 環境保護）

＿＿＿＿＿＿＿＿＿＿＿＿＿＿＿＿＿＿＿＿＿＿＿＿＿＿＿＿＿＿。

(4) He is pessimistic about the future.

（将来 /に関して / 悲観的）

＿＿＿＿＿＿＿＿＿＿＿＿＿＿＿＿＿＿＿＿＿＿＿＿＿＿＿＿＿＿。

(5) Yesterday, I had a discussion with Dad about work.

（仕事 /に関する / 相談する）

＿＿＿＿＿＿＿＿＿＿＿＿＿＿＿＿＿＿＿＿＿＿＿＿＿＿＿＿＿＿。

(6) Mr. Yamamoto is indifferent toward literature.

（文学 /について / 無関心）

＿＿＿＿＿＿＿＿＿＿＿＿＿＿＿＿＿＿＿＿＿＿＿＿＿＿＿＿＿＿。

Chapter 24

「〜に比べて」 Compared to 〜

There are a number of ways to compare things in Japanese, and 「〜に比べて」 is a commonly used structure for doing so.

> **Noun + に比べて**

1. 英語に比べて日本語の方が難しいと思う。
   Compared to English, I think Japanese is more difficult.

2. 今年の夏は去年に比べて雲泥の差がある。
   Comparing this summer to last year's (summer), there is a world of difference.

3. 昼間に比べて夜は映画館のチケットが高いです。
   だから、今行ったら安いです。
   Compared to the afternoons, movie tickets in the evening are more expensive.
   That's why if we go now, it'll be cheaper.

4. 踊りに比べて歌う方が得意です。
   More so than dancing, I am quite good at singing.

5. 日本に比べてアメリカの方が広い。
   Compared to Japan, America is bigger.

PRACTICE!

→Answer: P237

たん ご なら か ひと ぶん
単語を並び替えて、1つの文にしなさい。
Unscramble the following words to make sentences.

(1) It has rained more this year than it did last year.
あめ　　　　　おお　　きょねん　　　　ことし　　くら
雨　は　多い　去年　が　今年　に比べて

_____。

(2) His grades now are a lot better than they were before.
かれ　　　　よ　　　　　　　くら　　　　いぜん　　　せいせき
彼　は　良くなった　に比べて　以前　の　成績　かなり

_____。

(3) When compared to the tea-ceremony, the incense-smelling ceremony is not really known.
　　　　　　　　し　　　　　さどう　　　　　　こうどう　　くら
あまり　は　知られて　茶道　いない　香道　に比べて

_____。

(4) The Osaka-dialect is much faster than the Kyushu-dialect.
はやくち　おおさかべん　　くら　　　きゅうしゅうべん
早口　大阪弁　に比べて　九州弁　は　だ

_____。

(5) This product is much lighter than it was before.
じゅうらい　せいひん　　くら　　　かる
従来　製品　に比べて　軽くなった　この　は　かなり

_____。

84

Chapter 25
「〜につれて」&
「〜に従って / 〜に従い」

I. 「〜につれ(て)」 As 〜

This structure is used to show that as one thing changes, another thing changes along with it, and is often translated as "as... then..."

> Nouns that signify change
> Dictionary-form-verb ⟧ + につれて

1. 結婚する日が近づくにつれ、彼女は嬉しくなる。
   As the wedding day approaches, she becomes happier and happier.

2. お酒を飲むにつれて、カラオケが上手になる。
   As I drink more alcohol, I become better at singing karaoke.

3. 年を取るにつれて、記憶力が低下します。
   As one gets older, one's memory diminishes.

4. 時間の経過につれ、帰国したいと思う。
   As time passes, I feel more and more that I want to go home (to my country).

5. 会う回数が増えるにつれて、どんどん好きになった。
   As the number of times I met him increased, the more and more I liked him.

II. 「〜に従って / 〜に従い」 As 〜; In accordance with 〜

This structure is also used to show that as one thing changes, another thing changes along with it. It is the same as what we saw with 「〜につれて」, but also has another meaning that is often translated as "in accordance with〜"

6. 結婚する日が近づくに従って、彼女は嬉しくなる。
   As the wedding day approached, she becomes happier and happier.

7. 年を取るに従い、記憶力が低下します。
   As I drink more alcohol, I become better at singing karaoke.

8. 交通規則に従い運転しなさい！
   Drive in accordance with the traffic laws!

9. 大佐の命令に従って敵と戦いました。
   I fought the enemy in accordance with the colonel's orders.

10. ルールに従ってやりましょう。
    Let's play according to the rules.

擬音語

Japanese Onomatopoeia – "Crying 1"

【わんわん】 Cry in a loud voice; wail
   Ex. 弟はお兄ちゃんにおもちゃを取られて、わんわん泣いた。
   The little boy wailed after his older brother took his toy from him.

【おいおい】 Cry from extreme sadness or grief
   Ex. 彼はペットの犬が死んでおいおい泣いた。
   His dog died and he balled his eyes out.

【ぎゃあぎゃあ】 When a baby cries loudly
   Ex. 赤ちゃんがぎゃあぎゃあ泣き出した。お腹が減ったのかな。
   The baby started to cry loudly. I wonder if he is hungry...

たん ご なら か
単語を並び替えて、1つの文にしなさい。
Unscramble the following words to make sentences.

(1) As the night advances, the moon brightened up.

月 が 夜 が 輝いてきた につれて 更ける

_____。

(2) Let's dance along with the music.

踊り に従って 音楽 ましょう

_____。

(3) As science progresses, the wisdom of life is being lost.

生活の知恵 につれて 科学 が 失われていった の 進歩

_____。

(4) I put the bookshelf together according to the instructions.

組み立てた 本棚 に従い を マニュアル

_____。

(5) As the days passed, my sorrow grew.

経つ 悲しみ 月日 は 大きくなってきた が に従って

_____。

(6) As the typhoon approached, the wind became stronger.

近づく 風 が に従い が 台風 強くなってきた

_____。

Chapter 26
「～にして(は)」 & 「～わりに(は)」

I. 「～にして(は)」 For a ～

This next structure is used to describe something or someone behaving in an unexpected or unusual way, according to what we might normally expect. It can be used in both positive and negative situations.

When used with nouns, it is important to note that ～にしては can only be used with something that is specific, or something that gives the listener detailed information. When we are using a noun that describes something general, we can use 「～わりに(は)」 instead.

You may also be wondering how to know when you should or should not use the optional 「は」 in 「～にして(は)」. The 「は」, in this case, is simply for emphasis. In English, we add emphasis to what we are saying by accenting a word or string of words; "For someone who has only been studying Japanese for **three months**, you speak very well!" In Japanese, you can include the 「は」 for a similar effect. So, whether or not it is included depends on the feelings of the speaker.

Casual-form-verb Noun	+ にして(は)

1. バスケの選手にしては、彼の背はちょっと低いね。
   For a basketball player, he is a bit short.
   (Despite being a basketball player, he is a bit short.)

2. 漫画家にしては、絵がちょっと下手だね。
   For a mangaka (comic book artist), he is not very good at drawing
   (his pictures are a little bad.)

3. 外国人にしては、彼女の日本語は上手だね。
   For a foreigner, her Japanese is great. (Despite being a foreigner, her Japanese is great.)

4. 夏の日にしては、今日は結構涼しいです。
   Despite being summer, today is quite cool. (For being summer, today is quite cool.)

5. 女性にしては、彼女は強いですよ。
   For a woman, she is strong. (Despite being a woman, she is strong.)

6. 初めて卵焼きを<u>作ったにしては</u>、上手に出来たね。
  For my first time making tamago-yaki, I did a good job, don't you think?

7. 掃除していた<u>にしては</u>、あなたの部屋はまだ汚いね。
  Considering you cleaned your room, it's still a bit messy.

8. マリさんは今<u>ダイエットしているにしては</u>、よく食べるね。
  Despite being on a diet, Mari sure eats a lot, eh.

9. 日本語を1ヶ月しか<u>勉強してないにしては</u>、上手に話せるね。
  Considering you've only been studying Japanese for a month, you speak very well.

10. 彼は英語の<u>先生だったにしては</u>、彼の発音はあんまり良くないね。
  Considering the fact that he used to be an English teacher,
  his pronunciation isn't very good, is it.

II. 「〜わりに(は)」 Despite 〜

This structure is similar in meaning with what we just saw with 「〜にして(は)」. However, they differ in usage a bit. Whereas 「〜にしては」 is used with nouns that give specific information (like numbers, or dates), 「〜わりに(は)」 can be used for general terms, while 「〜にして(は)」 cannot. 「〜わりに(は)」 can also be used with adjectives, while 「〜にして(は)」 cannot.

Before looking at the example sentences, here are two sentences to demonstrate what I mean by "a noun that gives specific information" and a "noun that gives general information."

> Ex. 年のわりには、彼は結構元気だね。
> Despite his age, he is quite healthy/energetic.

Here, our noun is 「年」, which is the Kanji character for "year," but when you use it to describe a person, it means "old," as in "they have a number of years." But, in this sentence, we don't know *how* old the person is. It does not specify, so we cannot use 「〜にしては」. If we gave the age, we could use 「〜にしては」, however.

> Ex. ９０歳にしては、彼は結構元気だね。
> For a 90-year-old man, he is quite healthy/energetic.

Here, we are given the age (specifically) of the man. In this case, we can use 「〜にしては」.

Also, it should be noted that *even if* the information *is* specific, we still can use 「〜わりには」.

> Ex. ９０歳のわりに、彼は結構元気だね。
> For a 90-year-old man, he is quite healthy/energetic.

One more thing, please note that the Kanji form of 「〜わりには」 is written as 「〜割には」.

$$\left.\begin{array}{l}\textbf{Verb-casual}\\\textbf{い-adjective}\\\textbf{な-adjective}\\\textbf{Noun} + \textbf{の}\end{array}\right\} + わりに(は)$$

11. 年のわりには、彼は結構元気だね。
Despite his age, he is quite healthy/energetic.

12. １１月のわりに、今日はちょっと暖かい。
For November, today is rather warm.

13. 外国人のわりに、彼女の日本語は上手だね。
For a foreigner, her Japanese is quite good.

14. このラーメンは美味しい割には安い。
This ramen is cheap for how good it is.

15. 彼は暇な割に、助けてくれないって。
Despite not being busy, he said that he wouldn't help me.

16. 怠け者の彼のわりには、よく頑張ったな。
When you take into consideration how lazy he is, he worked quite hard.

17. 一生懸命勉強したわりには、不合格だった。
Despite studying as hard as I could, I failed.

18. 運動するのが嫌いなわりには、毎日ジムに通っている。
Despite the fact that I hate exercising, I go to the gym every day.

19. 漫画が好きなわりには、アニメはあまり好きじゃない。
Despite liking manga, I don't really like anime all that much.

20. 彼はちょっと太っているわりには、足が結構速いね。
Despite being a little chubby, he is quite fast.

Just like we saw with 「〜にして(は)」, the 「は」 in 「〜わりには」 is also optional, and is included to add extra emphasis to the perceived gap in what is expected versus the reality of the given situation.

PRACTICE!

→Answer: P237

（　　　　）内の単語を使って、1つの文を作りなさい。

Translate the following sentences into Japanese, using 「～にしては」 or 「～のわりに（は）」.

(1) For someone who lived in Japan, you don't really know that much about Japan, do you.
（住む / 知らない）

_____。

(2) Despite being unassuming/mild-mannered, she is quite strong-willed.
（控えめ / 意志）

_____。

(3) That is light for a sofa. I can move it by myself.
（ソファ / 軽い / 動く）

_____。

(4) Despite being quite careful, Mr. Watanabe is quick to misplace things.
（渡辺さん / 用心深い / 紛失する）

_____。

(5) Despite being cheap (in price), I think the quality is good.
（値段 / 製品）

_____。

(6) Even though I eat quite often, I don't get fat.
（食べる / 太る）

_____。

Chapter 27
「～（な）のに」 Even though, although

This structure is used to show that whatever is stated in the first clause of the sentence goes against what is stated in the second clause of the sentence; typically expressing something contrary or unexpected.

The structure is quite simple. The only thing we have to pay attention to is when we want to use this structure with a noun or な-adjective. In which case, we also need to append な.

Verb い-adjective	+ のに
Noun な-adjective	+ なのに

1. 一生懸命勉強したのに不合格だった！救いようがない馬鹿なんだ…。
   Even though I studied as hard as I could, I failed! I am a complete moron...

2. アメリカ人なのに"to lay"と"to lie"の動詞の違いが分からないって。
   Even though he is American, he still doesn't know the difference between the verbs "to lay" and "to lie"

3. 同僚は暇なのに手伝ってくれない。ずっと携帯を見てるだけ。まったくもう…。
   Although my co-worker is free (not busy) now, she won't help me.
   She just looks at her cell-phone all day. Gahhhh...

4. 「出来ない」って言ったのに、コーチにやらされた。
   Even though I said I couldn't do it, the coach made me (do it).

5. 風邪を引いているのに、彼はジムに行った。
   Even though he has a cold, he still went to the gym.

→Answer: P237

（　　　　　）内の単語を使って、1つの文を作りなさい。

Translate the following sentences into Japanese, using 「のに」 or 「なのに」.

(1) Ms. Nakamura is young, but she is quite mature.

（中村さん / 若い / しっかりする）

_____。

(2) Even though this hiking trail is really difficult, it's still popular.

（トレッキングコース / 過酷）

_____。

(3) Despite dancing to the best of my abilities, I was still laughed at by everyone.

（一生懸命 / 笑う）

_____。

(4) This book was written a thousand years ago, but it contains modern ideas.

（近代的 / 内容）

_____。

(5) Ginkaku temple, despite not being made of silver, is still called Ginkaku temple.

（銀閣寺 / 使う）

_____。

(6) I am being serious, but he won't take me seriously.

（真剣 / 真面目）

_____。

Chapter 28
「～しかない」 Nothing but ～

This next structure can seem a little confusing at first. It can be translated as "nothing but..." and is another way to basically say "only." Unlike 「だけ」 (the Japanese word for "only"), however, it can only be used with negative words.

When used with nouns, the structure is quite simple. We simply append しかない to our noun to get something like, "nothing but [noun]..."

Noun + しかない

---

1. 今、このバーには<u>男の人しかいない</u>…。別の所に行こうぜ。
   There are only dudes at this bar now... Let's go somewhere else, yo.

2. ダイエット中だから、今、冷蔵庫の中には<u>水しかない</u>。
   ジュースはもう飲まないことにしている。
   I am on a diet, so now there is nothing but water in my fridge.
   I'm making an effort to not drink any soft-drinks.

3. 私は小説に興味はない。私の部屋には<u>漫画しかない</u>。
   I am not interested in novels. My room only has manga (comic books).

4. アイスだったら、今、<u>バニラしかない</u>。ごめん…。
   If you want ice cream, we only have vanilla... Sorry.

Please note that in example sentence 1, we have to use 「しかいない」 and not 「しかない」 because we are talking about an living, animate thing. So, we have to use the ない-form of the verb 「いる」.

Of course, we aren't only limited to using only nouns. We can also use verbs. We just have to replace the 「ない」 of 「しかない」 with the ない-form of the verb.

<u>Noun</u> + <u>しか</u> + <u>verb's ない-form</u>

---

1. 日本語しか出来ない日本人は、海外でいい仕事を見つけるのは難しい。

   Japanese people that can only speak Japanese have a difficult time finding work abroad.

2. 私は、寿司しか食べたくない。

   I only want to eat sushi. (I want to eat nothing but sushi)

3. 彼女はアップル製品しか使わない。やっぱり、お金持ちだね。

   She uses nothing but Apple products. I knew it... she is rich.

4. 彼は足が細いからズボンしかはかない。

   His legs are skinny, so he only wears pants (so he wears nothing but pants).

5. 私は最近日本語の勉強を始めた。だから、まだカタカナしか書けない。

   I started studying Japanese only recently. So, at the moment, I can only write in Katakana.

擬音語 **Japanese Onomatopoeia – "Crying 2"**

【しくしく】 To stifle one's sobs and cry quietly
Ex. 女の子は迷子になって、しくしく泣きながら歩いていた。
The little girl lost her way and started sobbing to herself as she walked around.

【めそめそ】 To sulk; To cry from anxiety or fear
Ex. 彼は彼女にふられてから1ヶ月もずっとめそめそしている。
His girlfriend broke up with him a month ago, and he has been sulking ever since.
Ex. 彼は柔道の試合前になると、怖くなっていつもめそめそする。
Before every Judo match, he gets scared and always cries a little.

【ぽろぽろ】 Tears stream down one's face
Ex. その母親は、息子の無事を聞いて、ぽろぽろと涙を流して安堵した。
Upon hearing that her son was safe, the mother cried tears of joy.

→Answer: P237

（　　　　）内の単語を使って、1つの文を作りなさい。

Translate the following sentences into Japanese, using 「〜しかない」 or 「〜しか〜ない」.

(1) If you're going to do it, now is the time!

　（やる / 今）

_____ !

(2) I only have 100 Yen on me at the moment.

　（100円 / 持つ）

_____ 。

(3) You are the only one who can do this.

　（できる / あなた）

_____ 。

(4) This ring only has a little value (doesn't have much worth).

　（指輪 / 価値）

_____ 。

(5) You only have one birthday a year.

　（誕生日 / 1年）

_____ 。

(6) I have only ever been to Italy.

　（イタリア / 行く）

_____ 。

Chapter 29
「〜っぽい」-ish, -like

This next structure can be a little confusing, as it can be difficult to translate it precisely into English.

One usage of 「〜っぽい」 is to describe something as having a certain kind of essence or quality. In English we might use "-ish" or "like" to describe the same feeling.

Noun **い-adjective minus the い**	+ っぽい

1. 彼女はまだ若いけど、大人っぽいと思います。
   She is still young, but she is like an adult (adult-like).

2. 子供っぽい態度。
   A childish attitude.

3. そのビルは中国っぽいと思わない？パンダとドラゴンがいっぱい飾ってある。
   Don't you think that building just *screams* "Chinese?"
   It's decorated with tons of dragons and pandas.

4. 今日の朝からちょっと熱っぽい。風邪かな…。
   Since this morning I've been feeling a little warm/feverish. I wonder if I'm getting sick...

5. 目が青いし、背が高いし、金髪だし、彼はやっぱりアメリカ人っぽいね。
   His eyes are blue. He is tall. He has blonde hair.
   There's no question, he is very American-looking.

6. 安っぽいスーツ。
   A cheap looking suit.

7. この料理は油っぽくて美味しくなさそう。
   This food looks all greasy and not very good/appetizing.

8. 彼は学生っぽくありません。ひげまで生やしています！
   He doesn't look at all like a student. He even has a beard!

Pay attention to this structure when used with い-adjectives. The 「い」 from the adjective itself is actually dropped, like in example sentence 6. We don't say, 「安いっぽい」 or 「黒いっぽい」 we say 「安っぽい」 and 「黒っぽい」.

「〜っぽい」 can also be used with verbs to express that something occurs often.

Verb's ます-stem + っぽい

9. 私は本当に忘れっぽいです。
   I am extremely forgetful.

10. 飽きっぽい性格。
    A fickle personality.

11. 田中さんは最近怒りっぽくなった。
    Recently Tanaka has become quick to anger.

It is important to note that not *all* verbs can be used with 「〜っぽい」. Only verbs with nominal endings (動詞の連用形) can be used.

擬音語 (ぎおんご)

Japanese Onomatopoeia – "Saying 1"

【ごちゃごちゃ】 Saying various things
Ex. 「ごちゃごちゃ文句を言わないで、早く部屋の掃除をしなさい！」
"Stop whining. Now go and clean your room this instant!"

【ぎゃあぎゃあ】 Voice one's dissatisfaction or opposing view in a noisy manner
Ex. 彼は彼女の誕生日を忘れていたので、彼女からずっとぎゃあぎゃあ言われている。
He forgot his girlfriend's birthday, so she gave him a tongue lashing.

【くどくど】 The fed-up or bored feeling a listener (of some conversation) gets after being told the same thing over and over by the speaker.
Ex. 彼女は、彼氏の欠点をくどくどと話した。
She went on complaining about her boyfriend's faults at tedious length.

たんご なら か ひと ぶん
単語を並び替えて、1つの文にしなさい。
Unscramble the following words to make sentences.

(1) The criminal is said to have been wearing all black.

   き　　　はんにん　くろ　　　ふく
   着ていた　犯人　黒　は　服　っぽい　を　らしい

   _____。

(2) This coffee is watered-down and not good at all.

   　　みず　　　おい
   この　水　は　美味しくない　コーヒー　っぽくて

   _____。

(3) That actress is really sexy, don't you think?

   　　　じょゆう　　　　　　　　　　　いろ
   っぽい　女優さん　とても　あの　は　色　ね

   _____。

(4) Mr. Kobayashi has a really short fuse.

   おこ　　　たんき　こばやし
   怒り　は　短気　小林さん　で　っぽい

   _____。

(5) He gets tired of things fast and is the kind of person who doesn't finish what he starts.

   　　　かれ　　　　　　　　　あ　　　　　　　　ながつづ
   しない　彼　どんなことも　飽き　から　は　っぽい　長続き

   _____。

Chapter 30
「〜たびに」 Every time 〜

This structure is used when we want to express what happens *every time* as a result of something else.

> **Noun + の**
> **Dictionary-form-verb**] **+ たびに**

1. 私は旅行のたびにその国の小銭を持って帰る。いいお土産だと思う。
   Every time I take a trip, I bring home coins from that country.
   I think they make good souvenirs.

2. 彼女の顔を見るたびにキュンとする。
   Every time I see her face, my heart skips a beat.

3. インド料理を食べるたびにお腹をこわす。もう食べないほうがいい。
   Every time I eat Indian food, my stomach gets messed up.
   Maybe I shouldn't eat it anymore...

4. 試合のたびにすごく緊張する。
   Every time I have a match I get *super* nervous.

5. この曲を聴くたびに楽しくなる。歌手は誰ですか。
   Whenever I hear this song, I feel happy. Who is the singer?

In the first example sentence, we can see that we are pairing 〜たびに with 旅行. So, we must connect the two with the particle 「の」. When we do, we get something like, "Every trip..." and then go on to explain *what* happens every time. In example sentence 2, we have the verb 見る paired with 〜たびに. So, we do *not* need any particle to connect the two. We can simply say 「見るたびに」 to express "every time I see..."

→Answer: P237

「のたびに」を使って、2つの文を1つの文にしなさい。

Take the following sentences and combine them into one, using 「（の）たびに」.

(1) To go shopping. End up buying clothes.

買い物に行く。服を買ってしまう。

_____。

(2) To see him. Heart goes pitter-patter.

彼を見る。胸がときめく。

_____。

(3) Wash dishes. He breaks dishes.

皿洗い。彼は皿を割る。

_____。

(4) The changing of the environment. Creatures evolved.

環境の変化。生き物は進化した。

_____。

(5) To meet with Mr. Kato. Mr. Kato gets younger.

加藤さんと会う。加藤さんは若くなっていく。

_____。

Chapter 31
「～とたん(に)」 As soon as ～

Here we have an interesting grammar structure. In my experience, you won't find this used in daily conversation too often. But, it will definitely appear somewhere on a Japanese test. So, it is a good idea to familiarize yourself with it.

It is used to express two events, where one event happens immediately after the first.

> **Casual-past-tense-verb ＋ とたん(に)**

1. 彼の部屋に<u>入ったとたん</u>、具合が悪くなった。
   Upon entering his room, I felt bad/sick.

2. 彼女に電話を<u>かけたとたん</u>、彼女が出た。
   She immediately picked up the phone when I called her.

3. テレビを<u>消したとたん</u>、彼の子供が激しく泣きだした。
   Her child started crying hysterically as soon as she turned off the T.V.

4. 彼が作ってくれた料理を<u>食べたとたんに</u>、まずくて吐き出した。
   The food he made for me was so gross that I spit it out as soon as I put it in my mouth

5. 薬を<u>飲んだとたん</u>、元気になった。
   I felt better immediately after taking my medicine.

（　　　　　）に「とたん（に）」か「につれて」を入れなさい。

Fill in the (　　　)'s with either「とたん（に）」or「につれて」.

(1) As soon as he figured out that Mrs. Yoshida was not the president (of the company), he became cold and unfriendly toward her.

彼は、吉田さんが社長でないと分かった（　　　　　　　）そっけない態度を取った。

(2) As soon as I turned on the light there was a power failure.

部屋の電気をつけた（　　　　　　　）停電になった。

(3) As the internationalization process proceeded, various pieces of information started coming in.

国際化が進む（　　　　　　）色々な情報が入ってくるようになった。

(4) As soon as I began my climb up Mt. Fuji, the weather took a turn for the worse.

富士山に登り始めた（　　　　　　）天気が悪くなってきた。

(5) As I listened to her story, I became more and more interested in mountain climbing.

彼女の話を聞く（　　　　　　）だんだん登山に興味が出てきた。

Chapter 32
「〜うちに」During, while 〜

This next structure is used to express doing something before some change occurs or during a certain period of time.

Noun + の **Adjective** ない**-form verb** ている**-form verb**	+ うちに

1. <u>温かいうちに</u>食べてください。
   Please eat it while it's still hot.

2. <u>３０代のうちに</u>結婚したいと思っている。
   I want to get married while I am in my 30's.

3. お父さんは<u>元気なうちに</u>富士山に登りたいって。
   My father says that he wants to climb Mt. Fuji while he is healthy/able-bodied.

4. <u>寝ているうちに</u>人は夢を見るらしい。でも、ほとんどの人は起きた後すぐ忘れる。
   While sleeping, everyone dreams, but most people forget (their dreams) as soon as they wake up.

5. 新しい単語を<u>忘れないうちに</u>ノートに書いておいてね。
   Before forgetting (while you still remember) new vocabulary words,
   be sure to write them down in your notebook.

6. <u>眠くないうちに</u>宿題をしたほうがいい。
   You should do your homework while you are not sleepy (before you get sleepy).

（　　　　）内の単語を使って、1つの文を作りなさい。

Translate the following sentences into Japanese, using「うちに」.

(1) Within three years, I believe that I can save one million Yen.
（100万円 / 貯める）

_____。

(2) Please enjoy the food while it is hot.
（温かい / 召し上がる）

_____。

(3) I am going to go home while the traffic is light (before traffic gets heavy).
（渋滞 / 帰宅する）

_____。

(4) You should clean your room while your mother is in a good mood.
（穏やか / 片付ける）

_____。

(5) Before I die, just once I would like to go to Antarctica.
（生きている / 南極）

_____。

(6) While waiting for Dad to come home, I ended up falling asleep.
（帰る / 寝る）

_____。

(7) While this research was still a secret, it was able to progress.
（研究 / 秘密）

_____。

Chapter 33
「～ものか」 No way, as if

This is an expression we use when speaking casually. We use it to express a determination not to do something, or that there is no way ~ could ever occur. It is often translated as "as if."

> **Noun +** な
> **Casual-form-verb**
> い**-adjective**
> な**-adjective**
>
> **+** ものか

1. お前の言うことを<u>信じるものか</u>。
   As if I would ever believe anything you say.

2. 「最近の天気はどう？暑い？」「<u>暑いもんか</u>。雪まで降っているよ。」
   "How is the weather there? Hot?" "Hot? Are you kidding? It's actually snowing."

3. あの汚いレストランに二度と<u>行くものか</u>。
   I'll never go to that disgusting (dirty) restaurant again (for a second time).

4. 「この間の実験はダメだった？」「<u>ダメなものか</u>。成功したのだよ。」
   "Was your recent experiment a failure?" "A failure? No way. It was a success."

5. お前なんかに<u>負けるもんか</u>！絶対勝つぞ！
   As if I'd lose to someone like you! I'm definitely going to beat you!

6. 「元気ですか？」「<u>元気なものか</u>！一日中一生懸命働いていたよ。」
   "Doing well?" "As if! I spent the entire day working my head off."

7. 約束を破った彼を二度と<u>信じるものか</u>。
   As if I'd believe that promise-breaker ever again.

8. 「この映画は面白い？」「<u>面白いものか</u>。すごくくだらないよ。観ない方がいい。」
   "Is this movie good?" "No way. It's absolutely terrible. You shouldn't watch it."

9. 「田中さんはいい人ですね。」

「いい人なものか。いつも私の悪口を言っているらしい。」

"Tanaka is a good person, don't you think?"

"A good person? No way. He's always talking about me behind my back."

10.「君はこんな難しいことはできないでしょう。」「できないものか。見せてやるよ。」

"There's no way you can do something this difficult." "Oh, I can't, huh? Just watch me."

Please note that in really casual situations, it is common for「ものか」to be shortened to「もんか」.

Japanese Onomatopoeia – "Saying 2"

【ぼそぼそ】

To speak in a small, soft voice that is difficult for the listener to hear

Ex. あの先生はいつもぼそぼそと話すから、何を言っているのか全然分からない。

That teacher always speaks in such a soft voice, I have absolutely no idea what she is saying all the time.

【こそこそ】

To speak in such a way as to not be heard by others while expressing a negative opinion or thought

Ex. こそこそ悪口を言う。

To talk badly behind someone's back

【ひそひそ】

To speak in a soft voice so as not to be overheard

Ex. 子ども達は、お母さんへの誕生日プレゼントについて、ひそひそと話をしていた。

The children talked amongst themselves about what present they would get their mother for her birthday.

単語（たんご）を並（なら）び替（か）えて、文（ぶん）にしなさい。

Unscramble the following words to make sentences.

(1) No way is she prim and proper! She has a feisty, strong-willed personality.

清楚（せいそ）　！　男勝（おとこまさ）り　だよ　が　なものか　彼女（かのじょ）　の　性格（せいかく）

_____。

(2) No way can Fukuoka be considered the countryside. It is the third biggest city in Japan.

福岡（ふくおか）　だよ　都市（とし）　なものか　の　田舎（いなか）　で　。　が

日本（にほん）　3番目（さんばんめ）

_____。

(3) My foot is injured, so there is no way I can walk nimbly.

歩（ある）ける　のだから　足（あし）　軽快（けいかい）に　している　を　ものか　怪我（けが）

_____。

(4) Recently, in no way has Nagasaki been quiet/calm. There are people everywhere because of the festivals.

最近（さいきん）　賑（にぎ）やか　お祭（まつ）り　は　のどか　とても　の　長崎（ながさき）　なものか

。　で　だよ

_____。

(5) No way are kittens troublesome. They are absolutely adorable.

可愛（かわい）くて　鬱陶（うっとう）しい　仕方（しかた）　子猫（こねこ）　ないよ　が　ものか　。　が

_____。

(6) I don't disagree with you at all. I completely agree!

意見（いけん）　だよ　。　反対（はんたい）　きみの　に　大賛成（だいさんせい）　なものか

_____！

(7) There is no way I could say such a stupid thing to someone as strict as Mr. Yamada.

山田（やまだ）さん　そんな　言（い）える　ふざけたこと　を　厳（きび）しい　に　ものか

_____。

Chapter 34
「～ものだから/～もので」&「～んだもん」

I. 「～ものだから / ～もので」 Giving a reason

This structure is used when we want to give a reason or excuse for something.

> **Noun** + な
> **Casual-form-verb**
> い-adjective
> な-adjective + な
> 　　　　　　　　+ ものだから / もので

Please notice that when used with nouns, we must also add 「な」.

1. 彼女のお母さんとは知らなかったもので、失礼なことを言ってしまった。
   Because I didn't realize that was her mother, I ended up speaking rudely.

2. 風邪を引いているものだから、明日の会議には行けないかもしれません。
   Due to my cold, I probably won't be able to go to tomorrow's meeting.

3. 「なぜ遅刻したの？」「ごめん、目覚まし時計が鳴らなかったものですから。」
   "Why were you late?" "Sorry, (it's because) my alarm clock didn't go off."

4. バスケが下手なものだから、学校のチームに入れなかった。
   卓球部に入ってみようかな。
   Since I am no good at basketball, I wasn't able to make the team.
   Maybe I'll try-out for the ping-pong team...

5. 母が病気なものだから、海外旅行に行けなくなった。
   Because of my mother's illness, I couldn't go abroad (despite already having plans to do so).

6. 外国人なものだから、よく周りの人に日本語はできないと思われる。
   Because I am a foreigner, the people around me commonly make the mistake of thinking that I don't speak Japanese.

7. 暑いものだから、運動をしに出かけていない。ずっと家にいた。
   Because it's so hot, I didn't go out to exercise. I have been inside (my home) all day.

「ものだから」もしくは「もので」を使って、2つの文を1つの文にしなさい。

Take the following sentences and combine them into one, using 「ものだから」or 「もので」.

(1) She is shy. So, she can't quite adjust to her new environment.

彼女は消極的です。だから、なかなか場になじめない。

_____。

(2) It's strange. Whenever I hold this charm, I feel bolder and more courageous.

不思議です。お守りを持っていると勇気がわいてくる。

_____。

(3) It was obvious that she felt bad. So, everyone was paying attention to her.

彼女の嫌悪感は露骨でした。だから、誰もが彼女に気を遣っていた。

_____。

(4) It was really hard to say goodbye. So, we hugged each other over and over.

別れが名残惜しかった。だから、私達は何度も抱き合いました。

_____。

(5) I had a baby. That's why I want to go home early every day.

子供が生まれました。だから、毎日早く帰りたいのだ。

_____。

(6) Pardon me, I am in a hurry. So, I am going to have to excuse myself.

すみません、急いでいるのです。だから、そろそろ失礼します。

_____。

(7) This is the rule. That is to say, there is nothing that be done about it.

これは規則です。だから、仕方がない。

_____。

(8) The morning air is so refreshing. If you take some deep breaths, it feels even better.

朝はすがすがしいです。そして、深呼吸をするとより気持ちがいい。

_____。

II. 「〜んだもん」 Casual way to give reasons

Another form of this structure is a casual expression that is simply shortened to 「もん」. This way of speaking is often used by children because it sounds "cute." And because of its "cute" nature, it is also common for adults (typically ladies) to speak this way. When used by men, however, it is most often done in a sarcastic or ironic way.

This structure essentially takes on the meaning of 「から」, or "because," as it is used to give a reason/excuse for something.

> **Noun**
> **Casual-form-verb**
> **い-adjective**
> **な-adjective + な**
> } + **んだもん**

8. 「なぜ猫を飼いたいの？」「だって、<u>かわいいんだもん</u>。」
"Why do you want to have a cat?" "Well, because they're cute."

9. 「ちゃんと野菜も食べなさい。」「嫌だ。ブロッコリーは<u>嫌いなんだもん</u>。」
"Eat your vegetables like a good boy." "Yuck! But I hate broccoli."

10. 「また食べるの？」「だって、まだお腹<u>すいているんだもん</u>。」
"You're eating again?" "Hey, I am still hungry. What do you want me to do?"

11. 「また靴を買ったの？」「だって、<u>安かったんだもん</u>。」
"You bought *more* shoes?" "What do you want from me? They were cheap."

12. 「なんでいつも彼のことを聞くの？」「だって、<u>好きなんだもん</u>。」
"What are you always asking about him? "Because I like him."

13. 「やっぱり、お前は可愛いものが大好きだよね。」「だって、<u>女の子だもん</u>。」
"Man, you really like cute things don't you." "Yeah, well, I'm a girl after all."

The structures given above for how to use 「もん」 are "loose" at best. Because of its nature (being used by children and as a way to give an excuse), we are given a lot of leeway grammatically when using it.

For instance, in example sentence 13, after the noun 「女の子」 we have 「だもん」, not 「なんだもん」 (you can listen to the song "Ondedari Daisakusen" by Babymetal, one of my favorite Japanese bands, to hear this expression being used, which is actually where the inspiration for this sentence comes from). In fact, it is not uncommon to simply append 「もん」 and leave off the extra stuff altogether, like in example sentence 8. We could have also said, 「かわいいんだもん」, but the way it is written above is perhaps "cuter sounding," or, at least, more colloquial.

You may have also noticed that the word 「だって」 appeared numerous times in the above example sentences. When giving an excuse, it is especially common for children to start off by saying 「だって。。。」 So, when you hear this, you know right away that *some* kind of excuse is coming. It basically equates to "because," but when used to preface an excuse, it is kind of like, "Well, listen. It's because..." or "It's not *my* fault, because..."

Ex. 「なぜ彼を殴ったの？」「だって、僕のおもちゃを壊したんだもん。」
"Why did you hit him?" "Because he broke my toy."

The second speaker here is justifying their actions, as if what they did was completely normal and doesn't warrant discussion. "He broke my toy. So, naturally, I hit him... duh."

擬音語 Japanese Onomatopoeia – "Saying 3"

【ぺらぺら】　To speak smoothly or fluently.
Ex. トムは日本語をぺらぺら話せる。
Tom speaks Japanese fluently (smoothly, without pause).

【べらべら】　To talk a lot without thinking much.
Ex. 彼女がべらべら喋りまくるのには参ってしまう。
Her non-stop chatter annoyed me.

【ずけずけ】　To speak bluntly without considering the feelings of the listener
Ex. あの人は、相手の欠点をずけずけ言う。
That person just spouts off people's faults.

【ずばずば】　To give one's opinions without worry or holding back
Ex. 彼女はいつもずばずばとアドバイスを言ってくれる。
She always gives me honest advice.

【はきはき】　To speak in a loud, clear voice.
Ex. 「何て言っているか聞こえないので、もう少しはきはき話してください。」
"I can't hear what you are saying. Please speak up."

【ぶつぶつ】　To speak to oneself in a quiet voice. To complain about something.
Ex. お母さんは買わなければいけないものをぶつぶつ言いながら買い物に出かけた。
Mother muttered under her breath all of the things she needed to buy as she headed out to go shopping.

Ex. あの生徒はいつも先生にぶつぶつ文句を言う。
That student always talks badly about the teacher under his breath.

Chapter 35

「～恐(おそ)れがある」
There is the possibility of ～

This structure is used to express that there is a danger of something happening, and that there may be some cause for worry.

> **Noun ＋ の**
> **Casual-form-verb**] ＋ 恐(おそ)れがある

1. パンダが絶滅(ぜつめつ)する恐(おそ)れがあります。何(なに)かできることはないのかな。
   Pandas are in danger of going extinct. Isn't there something we can do?

2. このテレビゲームは若(わか)い人(ひと)に悪(わる)い影響(えいきょう)を与(あた)える恐(おそ)れがあります。
   あなたの子供(こども)には買(か)ってやらないほうがいい。
   There is the possibility that this game will have a negative effect on young people.
   It would be better to not buy it for your child.

3. このビルは古(ふる)すぎる。いつでも倒(たお)れる恐(おそ)れがある。危(あぶ)ない。
   This building is too old. It's liable to collapse at any moment. It is dangerous.

4. 飛行機(ひこうき)に乗(の)るのは安全(あんぜん)なんだけど、もちろん墜落(ついらく)する恐(おそ)れもあります。
   Flying in an airplane is safe, but, of course, there is still the possibility that it can crash.

5. 今朝(けさ)地震(じしん)が起(お)こったのですが、津波(つなみ)の恐(おそ)れはありません。安心(あんしん)してください。
   An earthquake struck this morning, but there is no danger of there being a tsunami.
   Please remain calm.

6. 心配(しんぱい)しないでください。あなたの病気(びょうき)は伝染(でんせん)の恐(おそ)れはありません。
   There is no need to worry. There is no danger of your illness spreading to others
   (it is not contagious).

7. 去年(きょねん)、持(も)っているすべての株(かぶ)を売(う)った。お金(かね)が全部(ぜんぶ)なくなる恐(おそ)れがあったから。
   Last year, I sold all of the stock that I owned because there was the possibility that
   I would lose all of my money.

Please be aware that the 「ある」 in 「恐(おそ)れがある」 can be conjugated normally. We can even make it negative, like in example sentence 6, to express that there is *no* danger of something happening.

（　　　　　）内の単語を使って、1つの文を作りなさい。

Translate the following sentences into Japanese, using「恐れがある」.

(1) This evening, there is the possibility of heavy rain.
（今晩 / 豪雨）

_____。

(2) If things keep going this way, there is a chance I will be fired.
（会社 / クビ）

_____。

(3) It is snowing, so there is the possibility that road surfaces will freeze.
（雪 / 路面凍結）

_____。

(4) When speaking that way, there is a chance that your meaning may be misinterpreted.
（言い方 / 誤解）

_____。

(5) If you don't get proper treatment, there is a possibility that it (your sickness) will come back
（治療 / 再発）

_____。

(6) There is the possibility that within a short amount of time, there will be a stock crash.
（株価暴落）

_____。

Chapter 36

「A ということは B ということだ」
「〜ことはない」
「〜ないことはない ／ 〜こともない」

I. 「A ということは B ということだ」 Because of A, it means B

This next structure is used as a way to describe two things (A and B) as being the same, or to use A as a reason for B.

1. 田中さんが入院しているということは、その仕事をするのは俺になるということだね。
   (A) (B)
   Seeing as how Tanaka is in the hospital, that means I'll be the one that has to do this work, eh.

2. パスポートを持ってないということは、君は海外に行ったことがないということだ。
   (A) (B)
   Since you do not have a passport, that means you have never been abroad.

3. 彼はダイエット中だということは、
   (A)
   私が作ったケーキを絶対に食べないということだね。
   (B)
   Seeing as that he is on a diet, there is no way he'll eat the cake I made.

4. 質問がないということは、みんな分かったということですね。
   (A) (B)
   Considering there are no more questions, that means everyone understands, yes?

5. 彼女は妊娠しているということは、もうすぐお母さんになるということだ。
   (A) (B)
   She is pregnant, so that means that soon she will be a mother.

→Answer: P238

「**A** ということは **B** ということだ」を使って、2つの文を1つの文にしなさい。

Take the following sentences and combine them into one, using 「A ということは B ということだ」.

(1) Mrs. Yamaguchi won't answer the phone. Mrs. Yamaguchi is busy.

山口さんは電話に出ない。山口さんは今忙しい。

_____ 。

(2) She received a ring. She was proposed to.

彼女は指輪をもらった。彼女はプロポーズされた。

_____ 。

(3) He was a con-man. I was tricked.

彼は詐欺師だった。私は騙された。

_____ 。

(4) The cookie that was here is gone. Someone ate it.

ここにあったクッキーがない。誰かが食べてしまった。

_____ 。

(5) You were born in the third year of the Heisei era. You and I are the same age.

あなたは平成3年生まれ。あなたと私は同級生。

_____ 。

II. 「〜ことはない」 There is no need to 〜

This structure is used to express that there is no need to do something, and is mostly used in spoken Japanese.

> **Verb's dictionary-form + ことはない**

6. あなたのせいじゃなかったよ。彼に謝ることはない。
   It wasn't your fault. There is no need to you to apologize to him.

7. 大丈夫ですよ。心配することはありません。私に任せてください。
   It's all right. There is no need to worry. Please leave it to me.

8. 一人ですることはないでしょう。誰かが手伝ってくれるから、きっと。
   There is no need to do it by yourself, right? Someone will definitely help you.

III. 「〜ないことはない / 〜こともない」 It's not that 〜

> **ない-form of Verb**
> **い-adjective** ⎤ **+ ことはない / こともない**
> **な-adjective** ⎦

9. 日本語を話せないことはないが、自信があまりない。
   It's not that I can't speak Japanese, it's just that I am not very confident in myself.

10. 寿司は食べないことはないですが、ラーメンの方が好きです。
    It's not that I don't ever eat sushi, but I prefer ramen.

11. 頑張れば、ＪＬＰＴの１級に合格出来ないこともないが、
    今回は2級を受けてみようと思う。
    If I were to work hard, it's not that I couldn't pass the level 1 JLPT,
    but this time I think I'll take the level 2.

12. このカレーは辛くないことはないが、もっと辛くしてもらえる？
    It's not that this curry isn't spicy, but would you be able to make it spicier?

13. <u>忙しくないことはない</u>が、あなたを手伝う時間はないです。ごめんね。

I'm not terribly busy, but I don't have time to help you. Sorry.

14. この携帯電話は<u>使えないことはない</u>が、新しいのを買いたいと思う。

This phone is okay (It's not that this phone is bad), but I want to buy a new one.

15. 今の仕事は<u>楽なことはない</u>が、一人で出来るはずです。

It's not that this work is particularly easy, but I should be able to do it by myself.

16. 「日本語が上手ね。」「いえいえ、<u>下手ではないこともない</u>けど…。」

"Your Japanese is great." "No, no, no, it's not bad, but..."

PRACTICE!

→Answer: P238

単語を並び替えて、1つの文にしなさい。

Unscramble the following words to make sentences.

(6) Everything will be fine, so there is nothing to worry about.

上手くいく　ことはないよ　何も　全て　きっと　から　気にする

_____。

(7) It's not like there is no hope, but I wouldn't get my hopes up.

あまり　希望がない　いいだろう　こともないが　方が　期待しない

_____。

(8) I'm not crazy busy everyday, but I am pretty busy.

毎日　そこそこ　ことはないが　目まぐるしい　が　忙しい

_____。

(9) It's not that I don't have an iPad, but I don't know how to use it.

使い方　分からない　を　ことはないが　が　持っていない　iPad

_____。

(10) It is not as if that plan is unreasonable, but I don't think we don't have enough people.

こともないが　その計画　人手　は　途方もない　と思う　が　足りない

_____。

Chapter 37
「たとえ〜ても」 Even if 〜

This next structure is used to express "even..." When used with a verb or adjective, it takes on the meaning of "even if [verb] / [adjective]..." When used with a noun, it takes on the meaning of "even [noun]" Then, the second clause of the sentence is typically some surprising or unexpected information.

たとえ ＋ Noun ＋ でも

たとえ ＋ 〔 Verb て-form / い-adjective て-form / な-adjective て-form 〕 ＋ も

1. たとえ暇_{ひま}じゃなくても、毎日日本語を勉強_{まいにちにほんごべんきょう}することにしています。
   If I am busy (not free), I study Japanese every day.

2. たとえ暑_{あつ}くても、彼_{かれ}はいつもジーンズを履_はいている。変_{へん}なやつだな。
   Even if it's hot, he always wears jeans. What a weirdo.

3. たとえ日本人_{にほんじん}でも、この漢字_{かんじ}の読_よみ方_{かた}は分_わからないよ。
   Even Japanese people don't know how to read this Kanji.

4. たとえ泣_ないても、チョコは買_かってやらない。
   Even if you cry, I (still) won't buy you any chocolate.

5. たとえ静_{しず}かでも、この町_{まち}に住_すみたくない。楽_{たの}しいところはないから。
   Even if it's peaceful, I don't want to live in this town because there aren't any fun places.

6. たとえ謝_{あやま}っても、彼女_{かのじょ}は許_{ゆる}してくれない。
   Even if I apologize, she won't forgive me.

It is also worth noting that in casual situations, we can drop the 「たとえ」 part of this structure altogether. For example, we can just say, 「泣_ないても、チョコは買_かってやらない」 or 「暑_{あつ}くても、彼_{かれ}はいつもジーンズを履_はいている」.

119

（　　　　）内の単語を使って、1つの文を作りなさい。

Translate the following sentences into Japanese.

(1) Even with Japanese food, if you eat too much you will get fat.
（和食 / 食べ過ぎ）

_____ 。

(2) Even if your kids are acting spoiled, you mustn't ever yell at them.
（生意気 / 怒鳴る）

_____ 。

(3) Even if it were just for a short time, I wanted to meet her.
（短い時間 / 会いたい）

_____ 。

(4) This must be done, even if it is completely foolish.
（ばかばかしい / やる）

_____ 。

(5) I like this hairstyle, so I don't care if people laugh at me.
（笑われる / 髪型）

_____ 。

(6) Even if the lecture is boring, I need to sit through until the end.
（講義 / 退屈）

_____ 。

(7) Even if that actor is famous in Japan, that doesn't necessarily mean that he is famous around the world.
（俳優 / 有名）

_____ 。

Chapter 38
「～にとって」
Concerning ～, to ～, for ～

This next structure is used to express a thought or feeling from someone's or something's perspective or point-of-view.

> **Noun + にとって**

1. 私にとってバスケは簡単だ。背が高いからかな…。
   For me, basketball is easy. I wonder if it's because I'm tall...

2. 中国人にとっては、日本語は簡単でしょう？文字が一緒だから。
   For Chinese people, Japanese is easy, right, because the characters are the same.

3. 子供にとってクリスマスはすごく楽しい時期です。
   でも、親たちにとってはやっぱり大変です。
   From children's perspective, Christmas is a wonderful time.
   But to parents, it is quite stressful.

4. 子供にとってこの番組は結構面白いらしい。
   To children, this show is supposed to be quite interesting.

5. アリゾナ人だから、私にとって日本の夏は全然暑いと思わない。
   I am from Arizona, so, to me, the summers in Japan are not hot at all.

→Answer: P239

（　　　　）内の単語を使って、1つの文を作りなさい。

Translate the following sentences into Japanese, using 「〜にとって」.

(1) This is a product that is gentle on the environment.
（自然 / 商品）

_____ 。

(2) When is a convenient time for you?
（いつ / 都合）

_____ ?

(3) To me, my father's older sister is my aunt.
（姉 / 伯母）

_____ 。

(4) For people who enjoy fireworks, the fireworks festival is an event that is very much looked forward to.
（花火大会 / 待ち遠しい）

_____ 。

(5) For me, it took a lot of courage to study abroad.
（留学 / 勇気）

_____ 。

Chapter 39
「〜からには」
Emphasizing a reason

This structure is used to express that something is obvious or self-evident. In the first clause, we give the reason for something that is obvious/natural/self-evident and in the second clause express some duty, obligation, estimation, or hope.

> **Verb + からには**

1. 彼女と約束したからには、彼女を助けないといけない。
   I made a promise to her, so I have to (am obligated) to help her.

2. 来年仕事でアメリカに引っ越すからには、英語を勉強しないといけない。
   Next year, because I am moving to America for work, I must study English.

3. 「できる」と言ったからには、彼は絶対に出来ると思うよ。彼はそういう人だから。
   He said, "I can do it." so I have absolute faith that he can. That is the kind of person he is.

4. 今年体重を減らすと決めたからには、高カロリーの食べ物を食べないで。
   You made a commitment to lose weight this year, so stop eating junk food.

5. ハーバードに入学したいと言ったからには、まじめに勉強しなさいよ。
   You said you wanted to study at Harvard. So, in order to do that, you must be serious in your studies.

「からには」を使って、2つの文を1つの文にしなさい。

Take the following sentences and combine them into one, using 「からには」.

(1) I decided to do it. I have to give it my all.

やると決めた。最善を尽くす。

_____ 。

(2) I have come this far. I cannot look back.

ここまで来た。後戻りできない。

_____ 。

(3) You do this kind of thing. Do you have any thoughts?

こんなことをする。何か考えがあるのだよね？

_____ ？

(4) You have become an adult. Take responsibility for your own actions.

成人になった。自分の行動に責任を持ちなさい。

_____ 。

(5) I got a scholarship. I must study as hard as I can.

奨学金をもらった。一生懸命勉強しなければいけない。

_____ 。

Chapter 40
「～はず」，「～はずがない」&「～はずだ」

I. 「～はず」 Must be ～

「はず」 has a few different structures with somewhat similar meanings. The first we'll look at is used to express a feeling of "should be..." or "must be..."

```
Noun + の
Verb
い-adjective          } + はず
な-adjective + な
```

1. 彼は何年も日本に住んでいるから、日本語が出来るはずだ。
   He has been living in Japan for a number of years, he should/must be able to speak Japanese.

2. 「今日、山田さんはご機嫌だね。」「うん、今日は給料日のはずだ。」
   "Yamanaka is quite full of pep today, huh." "Yeah, today must be payday."

3. 「これはいくらだった？」「分からないけど、高いはずです。ブランド物だからね。」
   "How much was this?"
   "I don't know, but I am sure it was expensive since it's a name-brand."

4. 長崎の魚の町は静かなはずです。田舎だから。
   Nagaski's Uono-Machi is most certainly a quiet/peaceful place. It is in the countryside.

5. 今日、田中さんはオフィスに来ないはずです。昨日、出張で東京へ行ったから。
   Tanaka shouldn't be coming to the office today. He left for Tokyo yesterday on business.

6. この漫画は面白いはずです。全ての若者が読んでいるから。
   This manga has to be good. All of the young people read it.

125

II. 「〜はずがない」 Couldn't possibly be 〜

Of course, we aren't only limited to using nouns, verbs, and adjectives in the affirmative. We can attach 「はずがない」 to the ない-form of these words as well.

> **ない-form ＋ はずがない**

---

7. 彼は何年も日本に住んでいるから、日本語ができないはずがない。
   He has been living in Japan for a number of years, there is no way he can't speak Japanese.

8. 自分で朝ご飯を作れないはずがないだろう。大人だよ、オレ。
   There is no reason why I can't make breakfast by myself, you know. I'm a grown man.

9. あの人が外国人でないはずがない。ほら、韓国のパスポートを持っている。
   There is no way that person isn't a foreigner. Look, he has a Korean passport.

10. 「彼は天才だから、分からないはずがない」。
    He's a genius, so there is no way he wouldn't get it.

11. このバックの値段が高くないはずがないでしょう。ブランド品だから。
    There is no way that the price of that bag isn't high, considering it's a name-brand.

12. アリゾナの夏が暑くないはずがありません。砂漠ですから。
    There is no way summers in Arizona aren't hot. It's a desert.

III. 「〜はずだ」 It's not wonder that 〜

This structure is used to express that something is patently obvious, and can be translated as "no wonder" or "it's not wonder that..." It is similar to what we say with 「わけだ」.

```
Noun
Verb
い-adjective       }  + はずだ
な-adjective
```

13. 眠いはずだ。一昨日から全然寝てない。
No wonder she's tired. She hasn't slept at all since the day before yesterday.

14. 暑いはずだ。エアコンが壊れている。
No wonder it's hot. The air conditioner is broken.

15. 日本語が上手なはずだ。彼は毎日日本語の新聞を読むそうだ。
It's no wonder his Japanese is so good. I heard that he reads the Japanese newspaper every day.

16. パソコンを開けないはずだ。パスワードが違っていた。
No wonder I couldn't open/access the computer. The password was wrong.

17. 生徒たちは嬉しいはずだ。雨で今日の授業は休講になった。
Of course the students are happy. Because of the rain, today's classes have been canceled.

We can also use 〜はずだ to express that something went against a prediction or expectation that we had. It can be translated as "supposed to be."

18. トムさんは3時に来るはずだったが、ここに来る途中で何か事件があったそうだ。
Tom was supposed to come at 3 o'clock, but on his way here, it seems there was some sort of mishap.

19. このラジオ壊れているかな…。このボタンを押せば音楽が流れるはずなんだ。
I wonder if this radio is broken... When you press this button it is supposed to play music.

20. 大学を卒業した後、すぐいい仕事が見つかるはずだと思った。

でも、やっぱりそんなはずはない。

After graduating from college, I thought I would be able to quickly find a good job.
But, now I understand that the world doesn't work that way.

21. 牛乳は体にいいはずだったが、最近の研究によるとそうでもないみたい。

Milk was supposed to be good for you, but according to some recent research it seems that it's actually not.

We can also use ～はずだ to express how our memory of something doesn't match the reality of some situation.

Verb's た-form + はずだ

22. 財布がない！バックに入れたはずなのに。

My wallet is not here! I could have sworn I put it in my bag. (It should be in my bag)

23. 机の上にあったはずのペンがない。誰かに取られたかな…。

The pen that should be on my desk isn't there. I wonder if it was taken by someone...

24. 彼女にメールを送ったはずなのに、なんで送信ボックスには何もないのだろう…。

I would have sworn that I sent her an e-mail, but why isn't there anything in my outbox?

擬音語 Japanese Onomatopoeia – "To fly / Jump"

【ぶんぶん】　A soft, quiet sound. The sound of a bug's wings
Ex. 蜂がぶんぶん飛んでいる。
The bees are buzzing around.

【ふわふわ】　Floating gently
Ex. 雲がふわふわ漂っている。
The clouds are gently drifting along.

【ぴょんぴょん】　To nimbly jump over and over
Ex. カエルがぴょんぴょん跳ねている。
The frog is jumping nimbly here and there.

128

PRACTICE!

→Answer: P239

もっと てきせつ
最も適切なものを1つ選びなさい。
Choose the right "はず-phrase" to fill in the blanks.

(1) Huh? The notepad that should be on the table isn't there.

あれ？テーブルの上に(　　　　　)のメモがない。

　　a. 置くはず　　b. 置いたはず　　c. 置いたはずがない　　d. 置く

(2) There is no way someone as diligent as he is would oversleep.

真面目な彼が寝坊(　　　　　)よ。

　　a. するはず　　b. しない　　c. するはずがない　　d. する

(3) This fish is an 'aji.' Now, 'aji' is in season.

この魚は鯵(　　　　　)。鯵は今が旬です。

　　a. です　　b. のはず　　c. のはずがない　　d. ですか

(4) In order to enroll at this college, a level of N2 or higher should be required.

この大学に入学するにはN2以上が(　　　　　)だよ。

　　a. 望ましいはずがない　　b. 望ましいのはず　　c. 望ましい　　d. 望ましいはず

(5) The students must all be frantic. If they don't pass this test, they cannot graduate.

生徒たちが(　　　　　)。この試験に合格しないと卒業できないらしい。

　　a. 必死なはずがない　　b. 必死はずだ　　c. 必死なはずだ　　d. 必死はずがない

(6) You'll recognize who Ms. Inoue is right away. She should be wearing really flashy clothes.

どの人が井上さんかすぐに分かるよ。彼女の服はとても(　　　　　)だから。

　　a. 派手なはず　　b. 派手なはずがない　　c. 派手はず　　d. 派手のはず

(7) No wonder it's chilly. The cooler is on.

道理で(　　　　　)。この部屋はクーラーがついている。

　　a. 肌寒いはずがない　　b. 肌寒い　　c. 肌寒いのはずだ　　d. 肌寒いはずだ

Chapter 41
Giving commands with 「～な」

This structure is as easy to use as it is useful. We can use this structure when we want to tell someone to *not* do something. We are already familiar with using the て-form to ask or request someone do something. Using ～な is essentially the opposite. Fortunately, this structure doesn't require any conjugation on our part. We simply append it to the dictionary-form of a verb to get "don't [verb]".

Dictionary-form-verb ＋ な

1. 泣くな！男でしょう？
   No crying! You're a man, right?

2. そんなこと言うな！
   Don't say such (awful/horrible) things!

3. 勉強しながら音楽を聴くな。気が散るでしょう。
   Don't listen to music while studying. It will distract you.

4. 妹を殴るな！
   Don't hit your little sister!

5. あんな派手な洋服を着るな！ピエロみたい。
   Don't wear such gaudy/loud clothes! You look like a clown.

It is worth noting that this structure is typically used by men. Women would typically use ～ないで, which doesn't sound as harsh or direct as ～な. Using the above sentences, a woman would typically say.

6. 泣かないで！男でしょう？
   No crying! You're a man, right?

7. そんなこと言わないで！
   Don't say such (awful/horrible) things!

8. 勉強しながら音楽を聴かないで。気が散るでしょう。
   Don't listen to music while studying. It will distract you.

9. 妹を殴らないで！
   Don't hit your little sister!

10. あんな派手な洋服を着ないで！ピエロみたい。
    Don't wear such gaudy/loud clothes! You look like a clown.

PRACTICE!

→Answer: P239

（　　　）内の単語を使って、1つの文を作りなさい。

Translate the following sentences into Japanese, using 「verb + な/ないで」.

(1) Don't do a dangerous thing like that ever again!
   （危険 / 二度と）

   _____。

(2) Don't play hooky!
   （ずる休み）

   _____。

(3) Don't just eat candy!
   （お菓子）

   _____。

(4) Don't ignore what I am saying!
   （無視）

   _____。

Chapter 42
「〜最中」 In the middle of 〜

This structure is used to express some event happening in the middle of another activity. It can be translated as "right in the middle of."

> **Noun ＋ の**
> **ている-form-verb** 　＋　**最中**

1. 運転している最中に電話がかかってきた。
   Someone called me as I was in the middle of driving.

2. 会議の準備をしている最中にパソコンを忘れてきたことに気づいた。
   As I was in the middle of preparing for the meeting, I realized that I had forgotten my computer.

3. 今、お母さんと話している最中だ。後で連絡するね。
   I am talking with my mother right now. I will contact you later, okay?

4. テストの最中に誰かの携帯が鳴った。
   In the middle of the test, someone's cell-phone rang.

5. 映画の最中に隣の人がずっと喋っていた。本当に頭にくるね。
   During the movie, the person sitting next to me kept talking. Isn't that just so annoying?

6. 私達のパフォーマンスの最中に停電しました。恥ずかしかった。
   There was a blackout right in the middle of our performance. It was so embarrassing.

7. 私は、今、教科書を書いている最中です。
   Right now, I am in the middle of writing a textbook.

8. お母さんは晩ご飯を作っている最中だ。
   Mom is in the middle of making dinner.

When we want to express one action happening in the middle of another one with this expression, please note that we use the particle 「に」, like in example sentences 1, 2, 4, 5, and 6. If we are simply describing someone or something in the middle of doing some action, we do not need 「に」.

→Answer: P239

（　　　　）内の単語を使って、1つの文を作りなさい。

Translate the following sentences into Japanese, using「最中」.

(1) When I went to Mr. Hayashi's house, he was in the middle of eating lunch.
（林さん / お昼ご飯）

_____。

(2) I am currently in the middle of investigating the cause.
（現在 / 原因 / 調査する）

_____。

(3) I'm sorry for interrupting your conversation.
（お話）

_____。

(4) You must never go outside during a typhoon.
（台風 / 外に出る）

_____。

(5) Currently, I am in the middle of applying for my visa.
（ビザ / 申請する）

_____。

Chapter 43
「〜って」 Quoting others

Next, we are going to take a look at how to quote someone in Japanese with 〜って. If you have studied other languages, you may have found that quoting what someone said can be quite a bit complicated. Even in English, it is a little tricky. For instance, if Misa says to me, "I am not going" and then later someone asks me where Misa is, should I say, "Misa said she wasn't going" or "Misa said she's not going"? In English, we have to change the tense of the verb so it matches that of the overall sentence. In linguistical terms, this is called "parallelism." Fortunately, we don't have to worry about any of that, because in Japanese we can simply use 〜って to quote someone, and don't have to worry about matching tenses or any other complicated grammatical matters.

Again, all we need to do is repeat what someone said and just append 〜って. If we append って to a noun or な-adjective, we must also append だ.

Verb **い-adjective**	]	+ って
Noun **な-adjective**	]	+ だって

1. 「みさはどこ？」「来ないって。」
   "Where is Misa?" "She said she wasn't coming."

2. 「なんでブランドンは東京に行きたくないの？」「高すぎるって。」
   "Why doesn't Brandon want to go to Tokyo?" "He says it's too expensive."

3. 「宮崎先生は何て言ったの、今？」「明日テストがあるって。」
   "What did Ms. Miyazaki say just now?" "She said that there was a test tomorrow"

4. 「田中さんは元気かな？今の仕事はどうだろうね。」「大変だって。」
   "I wonder how Tanaka is doing. I wonder how his new job is going."
   "He says it's a lot of work."

5. 「新しいスタッフは日本人？」「違う、タイ人だって。」
   "Is the new employee Japanese?" "No, she said that she was Thai."

<ruby>最<rt>もっと</rt></ruby>も<ruby>適切<rt>てきせつ</rt></ruby>なものを**1**つ<ruby>選<rt>えら</rt></ruby>びなさい。

Choose the right phrase to fill in the blanks.

(1) It says that the entrance fee is 800 Yen.

ここの<ruby>入場料<rt>にゅうじょうりょう</rt></ruby>は、（　　　　　　）。

a. <ruby>800円<rt>はっぴゃくえん</rt></ruby>って　　b. <ruby>800円<rt>はっぴゃくえん</rt></ruby>だって　　c. <ruby>800円<rt>はっぴゃくえん</rt></ruby>です　　d. <ruby>800円<rt>はっぴゃくえん</rt></ruby>らしい

(2) I hear that the Lion King show is absolutely fabulous.

ライオンキングのショーは（　　　　　　）。

a. <ruby>圧倒的<rt>あっとうてき</rt></ruby>って　　b. <ruby>圧倒的<rt>あっとうてき</rt></ruby>だって　　c. <ruby>圧倒的<rt>あっとうてき</rt></ruby>だったって　　d. <ruby>圧倒的<rt>あっとうてき</rt></ruby>です

(3) That's what I told you. She talks in circles.

だから<ruby>言<rt>い</rt></ruby>ったでしょう、<ruby>彼女<rt>かのじょ</rt></ruby>の<ruby>話<rt>はなし</rt></ruby>は（　　　　　　）。

a. <ruby>回<rt>まわ</rt></ruby>りくどいって　　b. <ruby>回<rt>まわ</rt></ruby>りくどいだって　　c. <ruby>回<rt>まわ</rt></ruby>りくどいらしい　　d. <ruby>回<rt>まわ</rt></ruby>りくどかったって

(4) Because of his hangover, he says that he is going to take the day off.

<ruby>今日<rt>きょう</rt></ruby>、<ruby>彼<rt>かれ</rt></ruby>は<ruby>二日酔<rt>ふつかよ</rt></ruby>いだから（　　　　　　）。

a. <ruby>休<rt>やす</rt></ruby>みます　　b. <ruby>休<rt>やす</rt></ruby>みです　　c. <ruby>休<rt>やす</rt></ruby>むって　　d. <ruby>休<rt>やす</rt></ruby>むだって

(5) Rumor has it that this book's ending is bad.

この<ruby>本<rt>ほん</rt></ruby>の<ruby>最後<rt>さいご</rt></ruby>は（　　　　　　）。

a. あっけなかったって　　b. あっけないだって　　c. あっけないです　　d. あっけないらしい

(6) They say that this cat has a cowardly personality.

この<ruby>猫<rt>ねこ</rt></ruby>の<ruby>性格<rt>せいかく</rt></ruby>は<ruby>少<rt>すこ</rt></ruby>し（　　　　　　）。

a. <ruby>臆病<rt>おくびょう</rt></ruby>って　　b. <ruby>臆病<rt>おくびょう</rt></ruby>だって　　c. <ruby>臆病<rt>おくびょう</rt></ruby>です　　d. <ruby>臆病<rt>おくびょう</rt></ruby>らしい

(7) My brother says he knows the answers to this quiz.

<ruby>お兄<rt>にい</rt></ruby>ちゃんは、このクイズの<ruby>答<rt>こた</rt></ruby>えが（　　　　　　）。

a. <ruby>分<rt>わ</rt></ruby>かりました　　b. <ruby>分<rt>わ</rt></ruby>かったらしい　　c. <ruby>分<rt>わ</rt></ruby>かっただって　　d. <ruby>分<rt>わ</rt></ruby>かったって

(8) This is not a cherry blossom, but a plum blossom.

この<ruby>花<rt>はな</rt></ruby>は<ruby>桜<rt>さくら</rt></ruby>じゃなくて、（　　　　　　）。

a. <ruby>梅<rt>うめ</rt></ruby>です　　b. <ruby>梅<rt>うめ</rt></ruby>らしい　　c. <ruby>梅<rt>うめ</rt></ruby>って　　d. <ruby>梅<rt>うめ</rt></ruby>だって

Chapter 44
「〜向き」&「〜向け」

I. 「〜向き」 Describing direction; Describing suitability

These next two structures are quite easy to confuse, so we will take a look at them together to help emphasize their differences.

First, we'll look at how to use 「〜向き」, which actually has two meanings. The first one is to simply describe the direction something faces or goes.

Direction + 向き

1. 東向きのアパートが欲しいです。
   I want an apartment that faces the East.

2. 僕はいつも右向きで寝ている。
   I always lie on my right side when I sleep.

3. 私のオフィスは北向きです。
   My office faces the North.

Another common use for 「〜向き」 is to describe something as being suitable or appropriate for someone or something.

Noun + 向き

4. その映画は子供向きではありません。
   That movie is not suitable for children.

5. この教科書は初心者向きです。
   This textbook is appropriate for beginners.

6. <ruby>夏<rt>なつ</rt></ruby><ruby>向<rt>む</rt></ruby>きの<ruby>洋服<rt>ようふく</rt></ruby>。

   Summer clothes.

7. ハリーポッターは<ruby>若<rt>わか</rt></ruby>い<ruby>読者<rt>どくしゃ</rt></ruby><ruby>向<rt>む</rt></ruby>きのシリーズです。

   Harry Potter is a series that is suitable for young readers.

8. アリゾナの<ruby>気候<rt>きこう</rt></ruby>はワイン<ruby>造<rt>づく</rt></ruby>りには<ruby>不<rt>ふ</rt></ruby><ruby>向<rt>む</rt></ruby>きだ。<ruby>暑<rt>あつ</rt></ruby>すぎるから。

   The climate in Arizona is not suitable for making wine since it is so hot.

9. <ruby>北海道<rt>ほっかいどう</rt></ruby>にある<ruby>全<rt>すべ</rt></ruby>ての<ruby>家<rt>いえ</rt></ruby>は<ruby>冬<rt>ふゆ</rt></ruby><ruby>向<rt>む</rt></ruby>きに<ruby>作<rt>つく</rt></ruby>られている。

   All of the homes in Hokkaido are well-suited for the winters.

10. おじいさんのため、<ruby>年配<rt>ねんぱい</rt></ruby>の<ruby>人<rt>ひと</rt></ruby><ruby>向<rt>む</rt></ruby>きの<ruby>携帯<rt>けいたい</rt></ruby>を<ruby>探<rt>さが</rt></ruby>している。

    "I am looking for a phone for my grandfather that is suitable for the elderly."

Please note how we can make our sentences negative by simply adding 「ではない」 after 「<ruby>向<rt>む</rt></ruby>き」 or by adding the character 「<ruby>不<rt>ふ</rt></ruby>」 before it. The character 「<ruby>不<rt>ふ</rt></ruby>」 is a negative-prefix that translates to "un" or "non."

II. 「〜<ruby>向<rt>む</rt></ruby>け」 Intended for 〜

This next structure obviously looks very similar to the one above, but they differ in meaning. We use 「〜向け」 when we want to describe what something is "intended for" or "aimed at," particularly in regard to products or services.

> **Noun + <ruby>向<rt>む</rt></ruby>け**

11. この<ruby>教科書<rt>きょうかしょ</rt></ruby>は<ruby>中級者<rt>ちゅうきゅうしゃ</rt></ruby><ruby>向<rt>む</rt></ruby>けに<ruby>書<rt>か</rt></ruby>かれている。

    This book is being written for intermediate level individuals.

12. <ruby>最近<rt>さいきん</rt></ruby>、<ruby>男性<rt>だんせい</rt></ruby><ruby>向<rt>む</rt></ruby>けの<ruby>化粧品<rt>けしょうひん</rt></ruby>が<ruby>色々<rt>いろいろ</rt></ruby>な<ruby>店<rt>みせ</rt></ruby>で<ruby>売<rt>う</rt></ruby>られている。

    Recently, various shops have begun to sell make-up for men (make-up targeted at men).

13. この<ruby>工場<rt>こうじょう</rt></ruby>では、<ruby>子供<rt>こども</rt></ruby><ruby>向<rt>む</rt></ruby>けの<ruby>洋服<rt>ようふく</rt></ruby>を<ruby>作<rt>つく</rt></ruby>っている。

    At this factory, they produce children's clothes (clothing intended children).

14. 最近、携帯向けのゲームが流行っている。
　　Recently, cell-phone games have become really popular.

15. 大人向けの映画だから、お前は観てはダメ。
　　This movie is intended for adults, so you can't watch it
　　(you are forbidden from watching it).

16. これは日本に行く人向けに書かれたガイドブックです。
　　This is a guide written for people who are traveling to Japan.

Remember, we use 「～向き」 when we want to describe the noun it is modifying as being *suitable* for something, and we use 「～向け」 when we want to describe the noun it modifies as being intended for or aimed at something.

擬音語 Japanese Onomatopoeia – "Light"

【ぴかぴか】 Intermittent flashes of light
Ex. クリスマスツリーがぴかぴか光ってとてもきれいだね。
The Christmas tree lit up and looked very pretty.

【きらきら】 To sparkle or twinkle.
Ex. 星がきらきらしている。
The star is twinkling.

【ぎらぎら】 To shine very brightly/strongly.
Ex. 夏の太陽はぎらぎらしている。
The summer sun is shining strongly.

【ちかちか】 A flashing or blinking light.
Ex. 部屋の電気がちかちかしているから、交換しないとね。
The light bulb in my room is flickering, so it seems I have to change it.

【あかあか】 Very bright light.
Ex. 晴れた日の朝日はあかあかとしてきれいだ。
The morning sunrise on a cloudless day is bright and beautiful.

【こうこう】 Light shines brightly (especially in the dark)
Ex. 暗い部屋の中で、ろうそくの明かりがこうこうとしていた。
The candle shone brightly in the dark room.

最も適切なものを1つ選びなさい。

Choose the right phrase to fill in the blanks.

(1) In this house, there is a large window that faces the South.

この家には（　　　　）の大きな窓がある。

a. 南向き　　b. 南向きけ　　c. 南を向いた　　d. 南

(2) This is a pamphlet for new students.

これは（　　　　）のパンフレットです。

a. 入学者向き　　b. 入学者向け　　c. 入学する者　　d. 入学者

(3) The person facing to the left right now is my wife.

今、（　　　　）人が私の妻です。

a. 左向き　　b. 左向け　　c. 左を向いている　　d. 左の

(4) Her advice was constructive and very good.

彼女の提案は（　　　　）で、とてもいいですね。

a. 前向き　　b. 前向け　　c. 後ろ向き　　d. 後ろ向け

(5) The current economy is on the rise.

最近の経済は、（　　　　）。

a. 下向き　　b. 下向け　　c. 上向き　　d. 上向け

(6) Please hang the picture so that it faces that way.

この絵を（　　　　）に飾ってください。

a. どこか向け　　b. あそこ向き　　c. あっち向け　　d. あっち向き

(7) Which direction will you face the desk?

この机は（　　　　）に置きますか？

a. どこか向け　　b. どこ向き　　c. どう向け　　d. どっち向き

Chapter 45
「～かけ / ～かける」
Half-finished ～

This next structure is used to show that something is only half-done, or was begun but never finished.

ます-form-verb + かけ / かける

1. 食べかけのパン。
   Half eaten bread / Unfinished bread.

2. 読みかけの本。
   A half-read book / A book that has yet to be completely read.

3. 書きかけの手紙。
   A half-written letter / An unfinished letter.

4. 飲みかけのビール。
   A half-drunk beer / A beer that has yet to be completely drunk

5. テーブルの上に食べかけのクッキーがある。
   There is a half-eaten / unfinished cookie on the table.

6. 机の上に書きかけのレポートが置いてある。
   There is a half-written / unfinished report lying in the desk.

7. 彼は飲みかけのオレンジジュースを捨てた。もったいないね。
   He threw away his half-drunk / unfinished orange juice. What a waste.

The above example sentences do a good job of showing what 「～かけ」 means and how it is used, but we are basically just using it to modify some noun. What kind of book? A half-read book. What kind of letter? A half-written letter. And so on.

We can also use this structure to describe situations where we begin to do something (but don't actually finish), are about to do something, or almost do something.

8. さっき、田中さんが何か言いかけたが、何も言わずにそのまま部屋を出た。

Just now, it looked as if Tanaka was going to say something, but he just left the room without saying a word.

9. 若いときに海で溺れかけたことがあったから、もう二度と泳ぎたいと思わない。

When I was young, I almost drowned at the beach. I have no inclination to ever swim again.

10. お風呂に入りかけたときに、誰かが玄関のチャイムを鳴らした。

Just as I was stepping into the bath, someone rang my doorbell.

11. 外で死にかけた子犬を拾って、動物病院まで連れて行った。

I picked up a puppy that was near-death and took him to the veterinarian.

12. 餓死しかけた猫に餌を食べさせてやった。

I gave the half-starved cat some food.

13. どうしよう、携帯のバッテリーが切れかけている。充電器持ってる？

Oh no, my cell-phone's battery is almost dead. Do you have a charger?

14. 映画を観かけて、寝てしまった。

I ended up falling asleep in the middle of the movie.

15. 私は病気で死にかけたことがあります。

I have almost died due to an illness.

たんご　なら　か　　　ひと　　ぶん
単語を並び替えて、1つの文にしなさい。
Unscramble the following words to make sentences.

(1) I am watching TV now, so please don't talk with me.

観ている　　かけ　　テレビ　　から　　話し　　今　　を　　ないで
み　　　　　　　　　　　　　　　　　　　はな　いま

_____。

(2) That was close! He tried to cheat me!

彼　　危なかった　　かけた　　騙され　　！　　に
かれ　あぶ　　　　　　　　　　　だま

_____！

(3) I am in the middle of reading this book, so please don't move my bookmark.

小説　　しおり　　読み　　だから　　ね　　を　　動かさないで　　かけの
しょうせつ　　　　　　よ　　　　　　　　　　　　　うご

_____。

(4) I was about to give up, but I did my best until the end.

途中で　　頑張って　　かけた　　投げ出し　　最後まで　　が　　やり遂げた
とちゅう　がんば　　　　　　　　な　だ　　さいご　　　　　　　と

_____。

(5) She was about to say something, but she left without saying anything.

去って行った　　かけた　　何かを　　言わずに　　彼女は　　言い　　が　　何も
さ　　い　　　　　　　　　なに　　　い　　　　かのじょ　　　　　　　なに

_____。

(6) There is some work I haven't finished, so I need to return to the office.

仕事　　が　　職場に　　ある　　から　　また　　かけの　　やり　　戻らなきゃ
しごと　　　しょくば　　　　　　　　　　　　　　　　　　もど

_____。

(7) I was deceived by how nice and sweet she looked.

優しさ　　かけの　　彼女　　惑わされた　　の　　に　　見せ
やさ　　　　　　　かのじょ　まど　　　　　　　　　み

_____。

Chapter 46
「～てならない」 & 「～てたまらない」

I. 「～てならない」 Extremely ～

This structure is used to express something in the extreme. It can be used with な-adjectives, て-form い-adjectives, and て-form-verbs. Please notice that when used with な-adjectives the「て」becomes「で」.

$$
\left.\begin{array}{l}
\text{て-form-verb} \\
\text{て-form-い-adjective}
\end{array}\right\} + \text{ならない}
$$

$$
\text{な-adjective} + \text{でらならい}
$$

Don't let the "て-form-い-adjective" confuse you. Below are some examples...

Ex.   楽しい → 楽しくて   暑い → 暑くて
      広い → 広くて   辛い → 辛くて
      寒い → 寒くて   苦い → 苦くて

1. 彼は試験に不合格してしまい、<u>悔やまれてなりません</u>。
   He failed the test and now he is extremely upset.

2. 北海道の冬は<u>寒くてならない</u>のです。
   Winters in Hokkaido are unbelievably cold.

3. 地震の後、お母さんのことが<u>心配でならない</u>。
   電話をかけてみたけど、出ませんでした。
   After the earthquake, I was worried sick about my mother.
   I called her, but she didn't answer.

4. 現代の若い人にとっては、携帯電話は<u>なくてはならい</u>ものだ。
   For the youth of today, cell-phones are an absolute necessity.

5. 彼女が言ったことが<u>不思議でならない</u>。
   What she said just now was absolutely bizarre.

6. 彼女に好かれているかどうか、気になってならない。
   I am dying to know whether she likes me or not.

II. 「〜てたまらない」 Can't get enough of 〜

This structure is similar in meaning to what we saw above with 「〜てならない」. However, this way of expressing something as being "extremely..." or "unbelievably..." is more casual and can be used when speaking with friends or people at the same or lower social status than you. Please notice that this structure can only be used with い-adjectives and that the たい-form of verbs are treated as い-adjectives.

> **て-form-い-adjective ＋ たまらない**

7. うちのワンちゃんは、かわいくてたまらない。本当に大好き。
   My dog is absolutely *adorable*. I just love him.

8. このゲームは楽しくてたまらない！
   I can't get over how much fun this game is!

9. 彼女についての噂を聞きたくてたまらない。
   I am dying to hear the gossip about her.

10. このケーキが食べたくてたまらないけど、今ダイエット中なんだ。
    I just want to devour this cake, but I am on a diet now.

11. アリゾナの夏は暑くてたまらない。冬に行った方がいいと思います。
    The summers are Arizona are absolute scorchers. I think it would be better to go in the winter.

12. 怪我した足が痛くてたまらない。病院に行こうかな。
    The leg I injured is killing me. Maybe I'll go to see a doctor.

13. 今日は暑い！冷たい水を飲みたくてたまらない。
    Man it's hot! I just want to chug some cold water.

14. 日本に行きたくてたまらない。
    I am dying to go to Japan.

15. みんなの前で転んで、恥ずかしくてたまらなかった。

I was totally embarrassed that time I fell down in front of everyone.

It is not uncommon for 「てたまらない」 to just be shortened to 「たまらん」. The meaning doesn't change. It is simply an even more casual way of speaking.

16. このケーキは美味しくてたまらん。

I can't get enough of this cake. (This cake is so good.)

17. 今日、暑くてたまらん。

I am dying from this heat. (Today is really hot.)

18. 日本に行きたくてたまらん。

I am dying to go to Japan. (I really want to go to Japan.)

Another interesting thing with 「たまらん」 is that it can sometimes even stand by itself to express "can't get enough of."

19. ともさんが作るパフェは美味しい。本当にたまらん。

The parfaits that Tomo makes are really good. I can't get enough of 'm.

20. この匂い…たまらん。

This smell... I can't get enough of it (because it is so good).

PRACTICE!

→Answer: P240

（　　　　　）内の単語を使って、1つの文を作りなさい。

Translate the following sentences into Japanese, using 「〜てならない」,「〜でならない」, or 「〜てたまらない/てたまらん」.

(1) Today is completely exhausting.
（しんどい）

_____。

(2) I have a strong feeling that something bad is going to happen.
（悪いこと / 気がする）

_____。

(3) Her death is terribly regrettable.
（死 / 無念）

_____。

(4) I absolutely hate that dog that was being mean to my cat.
（いじめる / 憎たらしい）

_____。

(5) Hot springs feel absolutely wonderful.
（温泉 / 心地よい）

_____。

(6) I can't help but think that this is not a coincidence.
（偶然）

_____。

(7) Her behavior is utterly ridiculous.
（行動 / 愚か）

_____。

146

Chapter 47
「〜ば〜ほど」 & 「〜ほど」

I. 「〜ば〜ほど」 The more you 〜, the more you ...

This next structure is used to express as one thing changes, the more another thing changes. It is commonly translated as "the more... the..."

> Verb's ば-conditional-form + dictionary-form-verb + ほど
>
> い-adjective's ば-conditional-form + い-adjective + ほど
>
> な-adjective + ならば + な-adjective + なほど

1. 日本語を勉強すればするほど、上手になるはずだ。
   The more you study Japanese, the better you should get.

2. ビールを飲めば飲むほど酔ってくる。
   The more beer your drink, the more drunk you will become.

3. 私は冬が大好きです。寒ければ寒いほど気持ちがいいと思います。
   I love winter. The colder it is the better I feel.

4. 暇ならば暇なほど生活がつまらなくなるでしょう。
   The more free (less busy) one becomes, the more life becomes boring.

5. 運転手さんがスピードを出せば出すほど車酔いした。
   The faster the driver drove, the more and more car sick I became.

6. 安ければ安いほどいい。
   The cheaper the better.

It is also worth noting that it isn't always necessary to use this entire structure. It is possible to drop the 〜ば portion of this structure altogether and just use the 〜ほど portion.

7. 「辛いのが好きですか。」「はい、好きです。辛いほどいいです。」

"Do you like spicy food?" "Yes, I do. The spicier the better."

8. 「どのサイズのコーヒーがいい？」「大きいほどいい。」

"What size coffee do you want?" "The bigger the better."

擬音語 Japanese Onomatopoeia – "Walking"

【うろうろ】 To go back and forth, not knowing what to do.
Ex. 道に迷ってうろうろしていたら、親切な人が道を教えてくれた。
After wandering the road, not knowing where to go, a nice person showed me the way.

【ふらふら】 To be unsteady. Not totally aware or conscious of what you are doing.
Ex. 酔っ払いがふらふら歩いている。
The drunk is stumbling around.

【ぶらぶら】 To walk around aimlessly
Ex. 暇だから、近所をぶらぶら散歩してきた。
I had nothing better to do, so I went for a stroll around the neighborhood.

【てくてく】 To walk with purpose (over a long distance)
Ex. 子供達は、毎日家から学校までてくてくと歩いて通っている。
The children walk for miles from home to school every day.

【とぼとぼ】 To walk in a downhearted fashion. To walk as if depressed.
Ex. テストの結果が悪かったので、彼はとぼとぼと教室を出て行った。
Because the result of the test was bad, he dejectedly walked out of the classroom.

【よちよち】 A baby unsteadily walks
Ex. 赤ちゃんがよちよち歩き始めた。
The baby started walking precariously.

【すたすた】 To walk briskly
Ex. 彼女は怒って、すたすたと部屋を出て行った。
She got angry and stormed out of the room.

II. 「〜ほど」 Comparing things; About; So 〜 that ...; As 〜

「ほど」 has a number of other useful structures. We'll take a look at some of them now.

The first use of 「ほど」 will be a little review, if you have read my first book. We can use it to compare two things.

> **[Object 1] は [Object 2] ほど〜ない**

9. 彼は俺ほど背が高くない。
   He is not as tall as I am.

10. 私は彼女ほど日本語が上手じゃない。頑張らなきゃ！
    My Japanese isn't as good as hers. I have to work harder!

11. アリゾナの冬は日本ほど寒くありません。
    Winters in Arizona are not as cold as winters in Japan.

12. 日本語は中国語ほど難しくないと思う。
    I do not think that Japanese is as hard as Chinese.

13. 彼ほど速く走れない。
    I can't run as fast as he can.

It is important to remember that when use 「ほど」, we need to end with the negative-form of our adjective or verb.

We can also use 「ほど」 to express an estimation, and has essentially the same meaning as 「くらい」.

> **[time expression] / [amount] ＋ ほど**

14. 駅まで２０分ほどかかります。
    It takes about 20 minutes to get to the station.

15. 1時間ほど彼を待っていた。
    I waited for him for about an hour.

16. 1年ほど日本語を勉強しています。
    I have been studying Japanese for about a year.

17. 彼は一人でピザの半分ほどを食べた。
    He ate about half of the pizza by himself.

We can also use 「ほど」 to describe an amount to which we cannot put a number.

> **Verb ＋ ほど**

18. お母さんは、今ちゃんと話せないほど怒っているよ。
    Mom is so mad that she can hardly speak.

19. 眠れないほど頭が痛い。どうしよう…。
    My head hurts so bad I can't sleep. What should I do...?

20. 彼は先月足を骨折したけど、今は歩けるほどに回復した。
    He broke his foot last month, but he has recovered to the point of being able to walk.

21. 一生懸命に日本語を勉強して、難しい漢字も読めるほどに上達した。
    I studied Japanese as hard as I could and learned how to even read difficult Kanji characters.

22. 牧さんは歩けないほど酔っている。やっぱり飲みすぎたんだ。
    Maki is so drunk he can't walk. Yup, he's had too much.

We can also use 「ほど」 to describe something as being the best, or the most ~.

23. <u>日本語ほど</u>難しい言語は絶対にない！

There is no language that is as difficult as Japanese!

24. <u>これほど</u>面白い映画を観たことがない。

I have never seen a movie as interesting/great as this.

25. <u>富士山ほど</u>綺麗な山はないと思う。

I don't think there is any mountain that is as pretty as Mt. Fuji.

26. <u>彼女ほど</u>怠け者はいない。

There is nobody on this planet that is as lazy as she is.

（　　　　）内の単語を使って、1つの文を作りなさい。

Translate the following sentences into Japanese, using 「ほど」.

(1) The more love and care you give to flowers, the more beautifully they bloom.
（愛情 / 注ぐ / 咲く）

_____。

(2) The more intense the experience, the more it remains in your memory.
（経験 / 強烈 / 記憶）

_____。

(3) The shinier a vegetable, the more fresh it is.
（野菜 / みずみずしい / 新鮮）

_____。

(4) The more classes you skip, the less likely it will be that you graduate.
（授業 / さぼる / 卒業）

_____。

(5) The more skillful/deft one's magic technique, the more interesting it is.
（マジック / テクニック / 巧妙）

_____。

Chapter 48
「〜て以来」 Since 〜

This structure is used to express how something has changed after a certain event or point in time. It can essentially be translated as "since." All we have to do is append 「以来」 to our verb's て -form to get "since [verb]ing..."

> **Verb's て-form ＋ 以来**

1. 日本に来て以来、毎日ラーメンを食べている。
   Since coming to Japan, I have been eating ramen every day.

2. 結婚して以来、ゲームをする時間がなかなかないんだ。
   Since getting married, I basically have had no time to play video games.

3. この本を読んで以来、すごくアメリカの歴史に興味を持っている。
   Since reading this book, I have developed a strong interest in American history.

4. あの店の寿司を食べて以来、お腹がちょっと変になっている。
   Since eating the sushi from that shop, my stomach has been a little upset.

5. 高校を卒業して以来、全然数学を勉強していない。
   Since graduating from high school, I haven't studied math at all.

6. 彼女と会って以来、他のことについて考えられない。
   Since meeting her, I can't think about anything else.

We can also use 「以来」 with nouns, as well. The noun should represent some point in time or event.

> **Noun + 以来**

7. 先週以来、彼と全然連絡を取っていない。
   I haven't had any contact with him at all since last week.

8. 誕生日パーティー以来、お酒は飲んでいません。
   I haven't had any alcohol since my birthday last week.

9. あの時以来、一度も東京に行っていない。
   Since that time, I haven't been to Tokyo even once.

10. 去年の事故以来、車に乗っていません。
    Since last year's accident, I haven't ridden in a vehicle.

擬音語 Japanese Onomatopoeia – "Personality/Character"

【さばさば】 To not worry about the small things, to go with the flow
Ex. 彼女は、さばさばした性格の人だ。
She is an open-hearted and easy-going person.

【なよなよ】 Someone seems unreliable or meek.
Ex. 彼はなよなよしていて、魅力的ではない。
He was acting rather effeminate; not very attractive at all.

【くよくよ】 To worry about things that cannot be changed.
Ex. 終わったことをくよくよしても仕方がない。
There is no sense in dwelling on the past.

【ねちねち】 Persistent, never satisfied
Ex. あの人はいつも色んな事に対して文句を言っていて、ねちねちした人だ。
That person is always complaining about something. What a fuss-bucket.

【うじうじ】 Indecisive, always hesitating
Ex. 「いつまでもうじうじしてないで、早く彼女をデートに誘ったら？」
"Quit being so wishy-washy. Why don't you just ask her out already?"

（　　　　　）内の単語を使って、1つの文を作りなさい。

Translate the following sentences into Japanese, using「以来」.

(1) I have not eaten mochi since New Years.
（お正月 / お餅）

_____。

(2) I haven't gone out with anyone since breaking up with him.
（別れる / 付き合う）

_____。

(3) Since graduating, I haven't seen my former teacher.
（卒業 / 恩師）

_____。

(4) The last time I went to Japan was for a business trip last year.
（行く / 出張）

_____。

(5) Since becoming pregnant, I haven't had any alcohol.
（妊娠 / 禁酒）

_____。

(6) Since that event occurred, it has been covered on the television news every day.
（発生する / 流れる）

_____。

Chapter 49
「〜に対して」
Toward 〜; In contrast to 〜

This structure is used when we want to express a feeling or an idea 'toward' someone or something. The 「て」 in 「〜に対して」 may be left off as well.

Noun + に対し(て)

---

1. 年配の方に対しては丁寧な話し方をしなければなりません。
   When speaking with the elderly, you must speak in a polite and dignified way.

2. 優しい本田先生に対し、生徒たちはいつも礼儀正しいです。
   The students are always polite towards the affable Mrs. Honda.

3. 永野さんはすごくいい人です。誰に対しても親切なんです。
   Mr. Nagano is a great man. He is kind to everybody, no matter who it is.

4. 彼の大統領に対する意見はよくないらしい。
   His opinion regarding the president is not a good one.

5. 世界史に対して興味を持っています。でも、数学に対しては持っていません。
   I have an interest in world history, but as for math, I am not interested at all.

6. 彼女は自分に対して結構厳しい。だから、子供たちに対しても厳しい。
   She is particularly strict toward herself. That is why she is also strict toward her children.

7. お客さんに対しては汚い言葉を使ってはいけません。
   You mustn't use foul language with customers.

8. あなたの意見に対して、一点言いたいことがあります。
   Regarding your opinions, I have something that I want to say.

9. 一般的には、日本人の外国人に対する意見はよいです。
   Generally speaking, Japanese people have a positive opinion of foreigners.

10. 田中さんは誰に対しても親切なのです。すごくいい人です。
    Ms. Tanaka is nice to everyone. She is a really good person.

Please notice how in example sentence 9 we use 「対する」 because we are modifying the noun 「意見」. We cannot say 「〜に対して意見」 because that would be grammatically incorrect.

Another use of this structure is express how two things differ. It has a meaning of, "A is..., but B is..." and is often translated as "in contrast to...," "while...," or "despite..."

Noun ＋ に対し(て)

Verb-casual ＋ のに対して

な adj ＋ な/である ＋ のに対して

い adj ＋ のに対して

---

11. 兄弟なのに、お兄ちゃんは大人しいのに対し、弟は結構うるさい。
    Despite the fact that they are brothers, the older one is quite quiet/mild-mannered, but the younger one is really loud/annoying.

12. 一般的に、日本の年配の人は大体演歌を好む。
    それに対して、現代の若者はポップスを好む。
    Generally speaking, older Japanese people like enka. In contrast to the younger generation of kids that like pop music.

13. 日本の冬は寒いのに対し、夏はとても暑い。やっぱり春と秋が一番だね。
    Despite the fact that the winters in Japan are so cold, the summers are quite hot. Naturally, spring and fall are the best.

14. 妻のアメフト好きに対して、私はサッカーが好きです。
    While my wife likes (American) football, I like soccer.

PRACTICE!

→Answer: P240

（　　　　）内の単語を使って、1つの文を作りなさい。

Translate the following sentences into Japanese, using 「対し（て）」.

(1) Despite being powerful militarily, that country's economy is weak.
（軍事力 / 経済力）

_____。

(2) This medicine is not effective against colds.
（薬 / 風邪に効く）

_____。

(3) My interest in Arizona has been piqued.
（アリゾナ / 興味が湧く）

_____。

(4) I spoke a little too harshly toward him.
（彼 / 言う）

_____。

(5) She was very polite and accepting of his rude attitude.
（無礼な態度 / 上品な対応）

_____。

(6) The people united and protested against the power of the politicians.
（権力 / 団結力 / 抗議する）

_____。

Chapter 50

「〜を込めて」 Full of 〜

This structure is used when we want to include some feeling or emotion into what we are saying. It can often be translated as "full of [noun]," where the noun will usually be a word to describe a feeling or emotion.

Noun ＋ を込めて

---

1. ボーイフレンドに愛を込めて詩を書いた。
   I put all of my love into the poem I wrote for my boyfriend.

2. 心を込めてこのバースデーケーキを作ってあげた。
   I made this cake for you with love.

3. 生意気な生徒が先生に皮肉を込めて返事をした。
   The cheeky/brazen student sarcastically responded to the teacher.

4. うちの子供が願いを込めてサンタさんに手紙を書いた。
   My child put their hopes and dreams down in a letter to Santa.

5. 全身の力を込めて本田選手がボールを蹴った。
   With all of his might, Honda kicked the ball.

6. 愛情を込めて、おばあちゃんがこのセーターを編んでくれた。
   With all of her love, Grandma knitted this sweater for me.

7. 誇りを込めてお父さんが私を抱きしめた。
   Full of pride, Father hugged me.

→Answer: P241

「を込めて」を使って、2つの文を1つの文にしなさい。

Take the following sentences and combine them into one, using 「を込めて」.

(1) Passion. To play the piano.
情熱。ピアノを弾く。

_____。

(2) Sadness. To speak one's lines.
悲しみ。その台詞を言う。

_____。

(3) Devotion. Made food.
真心。料理を作った。

_____。

(4) One's entire force. Hit the sandbag.
渾身の力。サンドバックを殴った。

_____。

(5) As a reminder to motivate me. I stuck the results of my failed test on my wall.
戒めの意。落ちた試験の結果を壁に貼った。

_____。

Chapter 51

<ruby>一方<rt>いっぽう</rt></ruby>

「〜一方だ」

More and more 〜; Worse and worse

This structure is used to express the continuous or on-going nature of something. It is most often used to describe something negative. It can be translated as "continue" or "more and more."

> **Dictionary-form Verb + 一方<rt>いっぽう</rt>だ**

1. アメリカに帰ってきて以来、僕の日本語のレベルは下がる一方だ。

   Since coming back home to America, my Japanese is getting worse and worse.

2. 歯が悪くなる一方だ。やっぱり歯医者に行かないと。

   My teeth are getting worse and worse. I really need to go to the dentist.

3. 日本語を勉強したい人は増える一方だ。アニメのおかげかな…。

   The number of people wanting to study Japanese is continuing to increase.
   I wonder if it's because of anime (the influence of anime).

4. 入院した後でも、お母さんの病気は悪化する一方だ。

   Even after being admitted to the hospital, Mom's illness is continuing to get worse and worse.

5. 日本の人口は減る一方だ。日本の政府はどうやってこの問題を解決するのか
   色々考えているようだ。

   The population in Japan is continuing to decrease. It seems that the Japanese government is thinking of various ways to solve this problem.

6. スキャンダルの後、彼女の人気は下がる一方だ。

   After the scandal, her popularity is continuing to fall.

7. 頭痛がひどくなる一方だ。病院まで連れて行ってもらえる？

   My migraine is getting worse and worse. Could I get you to take me to the hospital?

8. 携帯電話のせいで、交通事故が増える一方だ。

   Because of cell-phones, the number of traffic accidents is going up and up.

161

たん ご なら か ひと ぶん
単語を並び替えて、1つの文にしなさい。
Unscramble the following words to make sentences.

(1) This country's economic conditions continue to worsen.

いっぽう　けいき　　くに　　　わる
一方だ　景気　この国　は　悪くなる　の

――――――――――――――――――――――――――――――――――。

(2) I love manga, so my manga collection keeps increasing.

まんがほん　だいす　　ふ　　　　　　　いっぽう　　　まんが
漫画本　大好き　増える　だから　一方だ　が　漫画　が

――――――――――――――――――――――――――――――――――。

(3) He just kept apologizing. He wouldn't tell me what for.

りゅう　　いっぽう　　おし　　あやま　　　　　　　　　　かれ
理由　一方で　教えて　謝る　は　くれなかった　彼　は

――――――――――――――――――――――――――――――――――。

(4) As a result of global warming, temperatures continue to rise.

きおん　　ちきゅうおんだんか　　　　　　いっぽう　たか
気温　地球温暖化　は　一方だ　高くなる　で

――――――――――――――――――――――――――――――――――。

(5) All because of that worker, his rage kept building.

かれ　　ていいん　　　　　いか　　　　　　いっぽう　　　　　つの
彼　その定員　は　怒り　のせいで　一方だった　の　募る

――――――――――――――――――――――――――――――――――。

(6) His company's performance continues to decline.

かいしゃ　　　いっぽう　　　ぎょうせき　　かれ　かぶ
会社　は　一方だ　の　業績　の　彼　傾く

――――――――――――――――――――――――――――――――――。

Chapter 52
「〜によると / 〜によれば」
According to 〜

In Chapter 43, we learned how to use 〜って to quote someone. With this structure, however, we can express what someone else has said, without quoting them. This expressions basically translates to "According to ~"

1. <u>この記事によると</u>、2100年までには人間は絶滅しているらしい。
   According to this article, by the year 2100 human beings will have gone extinct.

2. <u>うちの母によると</u>、寝る前に酸っぱい物を食べたら悪夢を見るらしい。
   According to my mother, before going to bed, eating something sour will give you nightmares.

3. <u>天気予報によると</u>、明日は雪が降るそうです。
   According to the weather report, it is going to snow tomorrow.

4. <u>新聞によれば</u>、来月アメリカの大統領は安倍総理に会うそうです。
   According to the newspaper, next month the president of the United States will came to meet with Prime Minister Abe.

5. <u>昔話によれば</u>、地球は一匹の亀の背中の上に乗っていたそうな。
   According to an old story, the Earth is resting on the back of a turtle.

たん ご なら か ひと ぶん
単語を並び替えて、1つの文にしなさい。
Unscramble the following words to make sentences.

(1) If memory serves, I came to this river when I was little.

ちい ころ き きおく かわ わたし
小さい頃に　来たことが　記憶　あります　この川に　私の　によると

_____。

(2) According to what the children say, there are squirrels in this forest.

こどもたち もり はなし
子供達の　リスが　この森には　いるらしい　によれば　話

_____。

(3) According to what I have heard, he is a really serious and diligent person.

かれ き せいかく きまじめ
彼は　聞く　性格　ところによると　らしいです　生真面目な

_____。

(4) According to research results, garlic prevents cancer.

よぼう がん けんきゅうけっか
予防する　にんにくは　そうです　によると　癌を　研究結果

_____。

(5) Legends say that drinking water from this spring will grant a long life.

いずみ でんせつ の みず ながい
この泉の　伝説　飲むと　らしい　水を　によれば　長生きする

_____。

(6) According to calculations by AI, the Earth's average temperature will drastically increase.

あ えいあいけいさん へいきんきおん ちきゅう
さらに上がる　ＡＩの計算　平均気温は　によれば　地球の　らしい

_____。

Chapter 53
「～ところ」 & 「～たところ」

I. 「～ところ」 Just about to ～; In the middle of ～; Just when I ～

Now we are going to take a little crash-course on the various ways to use 「ところ」.

The first structure we'll look at is as a way to describe the time some action takes place.

> **Dictionary-form-verb**
> **Verb's ている-form**
> **Verb-casual-past-tense-form**
> **Verb-past-continuous-form**
> } + ところ(だ)

When used with the dictionary-form of a verb, we can express an action *right before* it happens. We get the meaning of "just about to [verb]"

1. 家を<u>出る</u>ところです。
   I am just leaving my house (just about to leave my house).

2. ランチを<u>食べる</u>ところです。食べ終わったら電話します。
   I am just about to eat lunch. After I have finished, I will call you.

3. 映画が<u>始まる</u>ところで映画館に着きました。
   I arrived at the movie theater just as the movie was starting.

4. 先生の質問に<u>答えようとしたところ</u>、田中君が答えた。
   Right as I was about to answer the teacher's question, Tanaka answered it.

If we want to describe an event as it is/was happening, we can use the present-continuous-form (～ている) with ところ(だ). It can be translated as "in the process of [verb]ing" or "in the middle of [verb]ing."

5. 私は今、日本語を<u>勉強している</u>ところです。
   I am studying Japanese right now. (I am in the process of studying Japanese.)

6. 電話がかかってきたときは、ご飯を作っているところだった。
   When the call came, I was in the middle of making food.

7. 明日のテストの準備をしているところです。遊ぶ時間はない。
   I am currently in the middle of preparing for tomorrow's test. I don't have time to play.

8. どんな文章を書けば良いか、今考えているところです。
   I am currently pondering what kind of sentence I should write.

9. お母さんが家に帰ってきた時、私は自分の部屋を掃除しているところでした。
   When my mother had come home, I was in the middle of cleaning my room.

We can also use 〜ところ with the casual-past-tense-form of a verb (the た-form) or the past-continuous-form (〜ていた-form) to express that we just finished doing something, or that we were *just* doing something.

10. 日本から中国に引っ越したところです。
    I just moved from Japan to China.

11. たった今、家に着いたところ。
    I just arrived at home.

12. お父さんが何かを買いに出かけたところです。
    My dad just left to go and buy something.

13. 「何か食べる？」「大丈夫です。ランチを食べたところです。」
    "You want something to eat?" "I'm okay. I just had lunch"

14. 「あ、田上くん！ちょうど君のことを話していたところだよ。元気？」
    "Hey, Tanoue. We were just talking about you. How's it going?"

To help me learn and understand a new grammar structure, I always try and think about what I am *literally* saying. This helps make clear in my mind *why* these structures take on the meaning that they do. In this case, I would think about how the word 「ところ」 by itself means "place." If we look at something like 「食べるところ」, which could be translated as "to be about to eat," we can see that, in this case, 「ところ」 isn't describing a physical space, but rather a space in time. 「食べる」 means "to eat," but it can also mean "will eat." So, I would think of 「食べるところ」 as literally meaning "will-eat-time," or "the time where I am going to eat." The same logic can be applied to

「食べているところ」, which could be translated as "is-eating-time." 「食べている」 by itself means "is eating," and when coupled with 「ところ」, we could translate it as something like "while-in-the-process-of-eating-time." Of course, in English, this is a very bizarre way of speaking, but it helps me make sense of what I am saying and makes it easier for me to remember. Maybe it will work for you to think of things this way.

All right, continuing on our ところ train, let's take a look at our next structure.

II. 「〜たところ」 As a result of 〜; Expressing a new understanding

This structure is used to express the result of having done something, or to express a new understanding after having done something.

15. 昨日の夜、あの店に行ったところ、もう閉まっていた。
   When I went to that shop yesterday evening, it was already closed.

16. 先月から毎朝ランニングしている。今日、体重を量ったところ、すごくビックリした！
   Since last month, I have been running every morning. Today, when I weighed myself, I was completely shocked!

17. 「屁の河童」というフレーズの意味を調べたところ、笑った。
   When I looked up what the phrase "he no kappa" meant, I laughed.

18. ネットで調べてみたところ、すぐに分かった。
   After looking it up online, I understood right away.

擬音語（ぎおんご） **Japanese Onomatopoeia – "Water 1"**

【びしょびしょ】 Soaking wet
   Ex. 傘を持っていなかったから、びしょびしょに濡れてしまった。
   I didn't have an umbrella, so I got soaked to the bone.

【ちょろちょろ】 The sound of a little bit of water flowing
   Ex. 台所の蛇口から水がちょろちょろ出ていた。
   Water was trickling from the kitchen faucet.

【ぶくぶく】 The sound of bubbles coming up
   Ex. お鍋の水がぶくぶくと沸騰してきた。
   The water in the pot bubbled up to a boil.

（　　　　）内の単語を使って、1つの文を作りなさい。

Translate the following sentences into Japanese, using 「〜ところ/〜たところ」.

(1) I just got out of bed.
（私 / 起床する）

_____。

(2) Dad came home as the children were going to bed.
（寝る / 帰る）

_____。

(3) Just as I was about to cross the crosswalk, a car came zooming by.
（横断歩道 / 渡る / 猛スピード）

_____。

(4) As I was thinking about him, I got a call from him.
（考える / 電話 / かかってくる）

_____。

(5) When I went to pay a visit to my uncle's house, he wasn't home.
（叔父 / 訪ねる / 留守）

_____。

Chapter 54
「～てからでないと…ない /
～てからでなければ…ない」
Can't ～ until you ...

This next structure is used to express that something can't be done until some other requirement is fulfilled.

Verb's て-form	+ てからでないと…ない
	+ てからでなければ…ない

1. 彼女を見てからでないと、デートしたいかどうか決められない。
   Until I see her, I can't say (decide) whether or not I want to go on a date with her.

2. 食べてみてからでなければ、他の人に勧めない。
   I can't recommend this to other people until I've eaten it myself.

3. この本を全部読んでからでないと、レビューを書けないでしょう。
   Until you've read the entire book, you can't write a review, right?

4. 彼と会ってからでないと、いい人かどうかは言えないでしょう。
   Only after meeting him can I say whether or not he is a good person.

5. ストレッチしてからでなければ、運動してはいけない。
   You mustn't workout unless you have stretched.

「～てからでないと…ない / ～てからでなければ…ない」を使^{つか}って、
2つの文^{ふた ぶん ひと ぶん}を1つの文にしなさい。
Take the following sentences and combine them into one, using
「～てからでないと…ない / ～てからでなければ…ない」.

(1) 手を洗^{て あら}う。おやつを食^たべる。
   Until you have washed your hands, you can't eat your snack.

   _____。

(2) 地盤を調査^{じ ばん ちょうさ}する。ビルを建^たてる。
   Unless the ground is surveyed, you cannot put up a building.

   _____。

(3) データを保存^{ほ ぞん}する。パソコンを閉^とじる。
   Until you save the data, do not turn off the computer.

   _____。

(4) しっかり点検^{てんけん}する。その車^{くるま}に乗^のる。
   You mustn't drive that car until it has been thoroughly inspected.

   _____。

(5) アンケートに答^{こた}える。あれをもらえる。
   You cannot get that until you have answered the survey.

   _____。

Chapter 55
「〜かわり(に)」&
「〜にかわり / 〜にかわって」

I. 「〜かわり(に)」Instead of 〜; In exchange; In addition to 〜

「〜かわり(に)」has a number of uses. The first one we'll look at is as a way to express "instead of."

> **Noun + の**
> **Dictionary-form-verb**] **+ かわりに**

1. 山田先生のかわりに私が今日の授業をしました。
   I taught today's class in place of Mr. Yamada.

2. 現金のかわりにビットコインを使えますか？
   Instead of cash, can I pay in Bitcoin?

3. 新しいパソコンを買うかわりに友達から中古のやつを買った。
   Instead of buying a new computer, I bought my friend's old one.

4. 自分で運転するかわりにタクシーで行くことにした。
   I decided to come by taxi instead of driving myself.

We can also use 〜かわり(に) with the dictionary-form of a verb to express doing something as a trade, or as a way of bartering.

5. 梓ちゃんに数学を教えてもらうかわりに、彼女に英語を教えてあげることになった。
   In exchange for Azusa teaching me math, I am going to teach her English.

6. お兄ちゃんの洗濯をするかわりに、お兄ちゃんは僕の部屋の片づけをするって。
   In exchange for doing his laundry, my brother says he will pick-up my room for me.

7. レストランまで運転するかわりに、友達にごちそうしてもらった。
   Since I drove to the restaurant, my friend paid for the meal.

8. 私は買い物に行ってくる。そのかわり、あなたはトイレを掃除しておいてね。
   I am going to go out shopping. While I am doing that, you can clean the bathroom.

The last structure we'll look at using with 〜かわり(に) is as a way to add more information regarding a certain subject. The detail in the first clause will usually be the opposite of or in contrast to the detail in the second clause.

9. このレストランはすごく高いかわりに、料理は超一流のシェフが作っている。
   The food at this restaurant is really expensive, but it is prepared by a world-class chef.

10. この辺りの家賃は安いかわりに、周りは結構うるさいんだ。
    The rent in this area may be cheap, but it can get rather loud.

11. この仕事は暇なかわりに、給料は少ないと思う。
    Because work is not very busy/difficult, the pay is not very high.

12. この薬はよく効くかわりに苦い。
    Although this medicine is bitter, it is quite effective.

II. 「〜にかわり / 〜にかわって」 In place of

In addition to looking at what we saw with 「〜かわり(に)」, 「〜にかわり」 and 「〜にかわって」 also have essentially the exact same meaning. We can use 「〜にかわり 」 or 「〜にかわって」 with nouns to express that something will act as a stand or replacement/representative for that noun.

Noun ＋ 〜にかわり / 〜にかわって

13. 私にかわって、山田先生が今日の授業をしました。
    Mr. Yamada taught today's class in place of me.

14. 料理が下手なお姉ちゃんにかわって、私が晩ご飯を作る。
    Instead of my sister, who is a terrible cook, I am going to make dinner.

15. 社長にかわり、副社長がアメリカへ出張します。
    In the president's (of the company) place, the vice-president (of the company) is going on the business trip to America.

16. 元々、ジェレミーが今日のスピーチをするはずだったが、病気で来ないらしい。
彼にかわって出来る人はいるかな…。
Originally, Jeremy was supposed to give the today's speech, but apparently
he's sick and not coming. Is there any capable person that can do it in his stead?

擬音語 Japanese Onomatopoeia – "Water 2"

【ぷかぷか】　Something light floating on top of water.
Ex. 池にアヒルが、ぷかぷか浮いていた。
The ducks glided across the pond.

【ぽたぽた】　The sound of large water drops falling slowly.
Ex. 雨漏りしているから、天井からぽたぽた水が落ちてくる。
Because of the leaky roof, large water drops are falling from the ceiling.

【たらたら】　Water or some other liquids continuously falling
Ex. 「コップからたらたら牛乳がこぼれているよ！ちゃんと真っ直ぐ持って！」
"You keep spilling milk from you cup! Hold it upright!"

【ぱしゃぱしゃ】　The sound of water splashing
Ex. 子供達は水たまりの上をぱしゃぱしゃと歩いた。
The children splashed as they walked through the puddles.

<ruby>単<rt>たん</rt>語<rt>ご</rt></ruby>を<ruby>並<rt>なら</rt></ruby>び<ruby>替<rt>か</rt></ruby>えて、**1**つの<ruby>文<rt>ぶん</rt></ruby>にしなさい。

Unscramble the following words to make sentences.

(1) Instead of my true feelings, I sometimes say what is expected.

<ruby>言<rt>い</rt></ruby>う　かわりに　<ruby>私<rt>わたし</rt></ruby>は　ことがあります　<ruby>建前<rt>たてまえ</rt></ruby>を　<ruby>本音<rt>ほんね</rt></ruby>の

_____。

(2) Instead of using a pot, I warmed it up in the microwave.

<ruby>鍋<rt>なべ</rt></ruby>で　<ruby>温<rt>あたた</rt></ruby>めた　かわりに　<ruby>電子<rt>でんし</rt></ruby>レンジで　<ruby>温<rt>あたた</rt></ruby>める

_____。

(3) Instead of remarkable economic growth, it is rapidly declining.

かわりに　<ruby>著<rt>いちじる</rt></ruby>しい　<ruby>早<rt>はや</rt></ruby>い　<ruby>経済成長<rt>けいざいせいちょう</rt></ruby>が　<ruby>衰退<rt>すいたい</rt></ruby>も

_____。

(4) He is a great worker/reliable worker, but he is too by the book sometimes.

<ruby>彼<rt>かれ</rt></ruby>は　<ruby>利<rt>き</rt></ruby>かない　<ruby>融通<rt>ゆうずう</rt></ruby>が　かわりに　<ruby>生真面目<rt>きまじめ</rt></ruby>な

_____。

(5) I get my protein from soybeans instead of meats.

タンパク<ruby>質<rt>しつ</rt></ruby>を　かわり　<ruby>肉<rt>にく</rt></ruby>に　<ruby>摂取<rt>せっしゅ</rt></ruby>している　<ruby>大豆<rt>だいず</rt></ruby>で　<ruby>私<rt>わたし</rt></ruby>は

_____。

(6) Nowadays, instead of New Year's cards, more and more people are sending their greetings by e-mail.

メールで　<ruby>人<rt>ひと</rt></ruby>が　<ruby>年賀状<rt>ねんがじょう</rt></ruby>に　<ruby>増<rt>ふ</rt></ruby>えてきた　<ruby>新年<rt>しんねん</rt></ruby>の　かわって　<ruby>昨今<rt>さっこん</rt></ruby>は
<ruby>挨拶<rt>あいさつ</rt></ruby>をする

_____。

Chapter 56
「～だけ」 Expressing degrees or limits

Certainly, you have already seen the word 「だけ」 numerous times. One meaning it has is "only," but it can also be used with verbs, い-adjectives, and な-adjectives to express a degree or limit.

Noun		
Verb	+ だけ	
い-adjective		
な-adjective	+ なだけ	

1. 使いたいだけ使っていいですよ。今、私は使わないから。
   I don't need it now, so you can use it all you want.

2. 毎日できるだけ日本語を勉強します。
   I will study study Japanese as much as I can every day.

3. たった2分遅刻しただけだよ。それだけでクビになっちゃった…。厳しいな。
   I was only two minutes late, man. And just for that I was fired... unreal.

4. 好きなテレビ番組を見たかったら、できるだけ早く家に帰った。
   I rushed home as fast as I could so I could catch my favorite T.V. Show.

5. お金を欲しいだけ持っているからといって、幸せだとは限らないです。
   やっぱり一番大事なのは健康だと思います。
   Having more money than you can spend doesn't necessarily mean you are happy.
   The most important thing is your health.

6. 彼はいつも口先だけだ。
   Everything he says is just all talk.

PRACTICE!

→Answer: P241

（　　　　　）に「だけ」か「なだけ」を入れなさい。
Fill in the (　　　)'s with either「だけ」or「なだけ」.

(1) He sees people only for their positions in society.
彼は肩書（　　　　　　　）で人を見る。

(2) All she did was complain, and, in the end, didn't help us at all.
彼女は愚痴を言う（　　　　　　　）で、結局のところ何も手伝ってくれなかった。

(3) This building is just old and isn't worth much.
この建物はただ古い（　　　　　　）で、あまり価値はない。

(4) Mr. Sakamoto is not only reasonable, but wise as well.
坂本さんは理性的（　　　　　　）ではなく、聡明でもある。

擬音語 **Japanese Onomatopoeia – "To sleep"**

【うとうと】　　　When starting to fall asleep
　　　　　　　　Ex. お父さんがうとうとしながらテレビを観ている。
　　　　　　　　Dad is dozing off as he watches TV.

【すやすや】　　　Sleeping soundly
　　　　　　　　Ex. 赤ちゃんがベッドですやすやお昼寝をしている。
　　　　　　　　The baby is soundly sleeping as he naps in bed.

【ぐーぐー】　　　To snore while sleeping
　　　　　　　　Ex. お父さんがぐーぐーソファで寝ている。
　　　　　　　　Dad is snoring as he sleeps on the couch.

【こっくりこっくり】　To be nodding off; dozing
　　　　　　　　Ex. 授業中、こっくりこっくりしていたら、先生に注意された。
　　　　　　　　I was admonished by the teacher for nodding off during class.

Chapter 57
「ばかり」

I. 「〜ばかり」 Just 〜; Only 〜; Continue to 〜; On account of 〜

「ばかり」 has a number of uses. The first one we'll look at is used to describe an action that *just* finished.

> ### た-form Verb ＋ ばかり

1. 歯を磨いたばかりだから、オレンジジュースを飲みたくない。
   I just brushed my teeth, so I don't want to have any orange juice.

2. ご飯を食べたばかりなので、泳ぎに行くのは３０分ほど待たないといけない。
   I just finished eating, so I have to wait 30 minutes before I can go swimming.

3. 買ったばかりの携帯を失くしてしまった。どこにあるんだろう…。
   I lost the phone that I *just* bought. Where could it be...?

4. あの本は読んだばかりだから、よく話を覚えているよ。
   I just finished reading that book, so I remember/know the story quite well.

5. 買ったばかりの車だから、まだスムーズに運転できない。まだ慣れてないから。
   I just bought this car, so I'm not able to drive it very smoothly yet.
   I still haven't gotten used to it.

The next use of 「ばかり」 that we'll look at is to express "only," or "nothing but."

> ### Dictionary-form-verb ＋ ばかり いる

6. 彼女は体にいいものばかり食べます。
   She is so into health that she only ever eats foods that are good for you.

7. テレビばかり見ないで！ちゃんと宿題をしなさい！
   "Don't just watch T.V. All day! Do your homework! (like you should)"

8. 飴を食べてばかりいるな！
   Don't just eat nothing but candy!

9. ゲームばかりしていたら、成績が悪くなる。
   If you do nothing but play games, your grades will suffer (become bad).

10. 飛行機で隣に座っていた赤ちゃんが泣いてばかりいた。最悪だった…。
    On the plane, the baby that was sitting next to me cried the whole time (did nothing but cry). It was horrible...

11. 漫画ばかり読まないで、ちゃんとした小説を読んだら？
    Don't just read manga. How about reading an actual novel?

Another use of 「ばかり」 is to express the continuation of some action.

Dictionary-form-verb ＋ ばかり

12. アメリカに帰国してから、僕の日本語は低下するばかりだ。
    Since moving back to America, my Japanese keeps/continues to get worse.

13. おじいちゃんの病気は悪くなるばかりだ。できることは本当にないの？
    Grandpa's sickness keeps getting worse. Is there really nothing they can do?

14. 携帯電話は普及するばかりだ。うちの母までアイフォンを持っている。
    Cell-phones are continuing to become more prominent. Even my mother has an iPhone.

15. このドラマは面白くなるばかりだ。すごく好き。
    This drama keeps getting more and more interesting. I really like it.

16. 日本語を勉強する人は増えるばかりだ。アニメのせいかな…。
    The number of people studying Japanese is continuing to increase.
    I wonder if is because of anime...

178

The next 「ばかり」 structure we'll look at is used to express "on account of," "because," or "for the sole reason."

た-form-verb い-adjective な-adjective ＋ な/である Noun ＋ （である）	＋ ばかりに

17. たった2分遅刻したばかりに、クビになっちゃった。
    Just because I was two minutes late, I was fired.

18. 背が高いばかりに、バスケが得意とよく思われる。本当は全然上手じゃない。
    On account of me being tall, people often think I am good at basketball.
    In reality, I am not good at all.

19. 彼は外国人であるばかりに、日本語はできないとよく思われる。
    Just because he is a foreigner, people often think that he can't speak Japanese.

20. 彼女は美人なばかりに、よくモデルにスカウトされる。
    On account of the fact that she is beautiful, she is often scouted to be a model.

21. スタバのスタッフが可愛いと言い出したばかりに、彼女に怒られた。
    Because I commented that the worker at the Starbucks was cute, my girlfriend got mad at me.

22. この店の食べ物はあまり美味しくないけど、店員が可愛いばかりに
    お客さんがいつもいる。
    This place's food isn't really very good, but because the stuff is cute there are always customers.

II. 「〜とばかりに」 As if 〜; As though 〜

This structure typically translates to "as if" or "as though," and is used to express how something appeared to be (whether or not it is true).

```
Verb-phrase
Noun                    + とばかりに
い-adjective
な-adjective
```

23. 泣き出しそうとばかりに、彼女が部屋を飛び出した。
    As if she were about to start crying, she ran out of the room.

24. 彼はそのカレーを食べたとき、死にそうとばかりにごくごくと水を飲んでいた。
    When he ate that curry, he was gulping down water like he was dying.

25. 私の話は全然面白くないとばかりに、彼女はあくびをしました。
    As though my story were completely uninteresting, she yawned.

26. 僕たちが彼らに負けたのは僕のせいとばかりに、誰も僕と話さなかった。
    Nobody would talk to me, as though us losing to them was my fault.

27. とても簡単とばかりに、彼は一人でやり始めた。
    Acting as if it were really easy, he started to do it by himself.

28. 「行かないで！」と言わんばかりに、子犬が私を見つめていた。
    As if to say "don't go!" my puppy gazed at me.

擬音語　Japanese Onomatopoeia – "Sticky"

【ねばねば】　Something has adhesive and is easy to stick to something
　　　　　　　Ex. 納豆はねばねばしている。
　　　　　　　Natto is sticky.

【べたべた】　Objects fit together perfectly or snugly
【べとべと】　Ex. 汗でシャツがべたべたとくっつく。
　　　　　　　My shirt sticks to me because of the sweat.
　　　　　　　Ex. バターで手がべとべとする。
　　　　　　　My hands are covered in butter. (the butter is sticking to my hands)

<ruby>最<rt>もっと</rt></ruby>も<ruby>適切<rt>てきせつ</rt></ruby>なものを<ruby>1<rt>ひと</rt></ruby>つ<ruby>選<rt>えら</rt></ruby>びなさい。

Choose the right "ばかり-phrase" to fill in the blanks.

(1) I spilled soy sauce on my freshly washed clothes.

<ruby>洗濯<rt>せんたく</rt></ruby>し＿＿＿＿＿なのに、<ruby>醤油<rt>しょうゆ</rt></ruby>を<ruby>洋服<rt>ようふく</rt></ruby>にこぼしてしまった。

    a. ばかり   b. たばかり   c. るばかり   d. ばかりに

(2) Mr. Shimizu is always lazing about.

<ruby>清水<rt>しみず</rt></ruby>さんは<ruby>怠<rt>なま</rt></ruby>けて＿＿＿＿＿いる。

    a. ばかり   b. たばかり   c. るばかり   d. とばかりに

(3) At that time, France was only expanding its colonies.

<ruby>当時<rt>とうじ</rt></ruby>、フランスは<ruby>殖民地<rt>しょくみんち</rt></ruby>を<ruby>拡大<rt>かくだい</rt></ruby>＿＿＿＿＿だった。

    a. ばかり   b. したばかり   c. するばかり   d. とばかりに

(4) It was clear, based solely on their accent, that they were from Kyushu.

<ruby>言葉<rt>ことば</rt></ruby>がなまってい＿＿＿＿＿<ruby>九州出身<rt>きゅうしゅうしゅっしん</rt></ruby>だとすぐにばれた。

    a. ばかり   b. たばかり   c. ばかりに   d. とばかりに

(5) Even though natto is very nutritious, just because of its smell, people don't like it.

<ruby>納豆<rt>なっとう</rt></ruby>は<ruby>栄養<rt>えいよう</rt></ruby>が<ruby>豊富<rt>ほうふ</rt></ruby>なのに<ruby>臭<rt>くさ</rt></ruby>い＿＿＿＿＿<ruby>嫌<rt>きら</rt></ruby>われる。

    a. ばかり   b. たばかり   c. ばかりに   d. とばかりに

(6) Because that student was immature, he said something rude to the professor.

その<ruby>学生<rt>がくせい</rt></ruby>は<ruby>未熟<rt>みじゅく</rt></ruby>で＿＿＿＿＿、<ruby>教授<rt>きょうじゅ</rt></ruby>に<ruby>失礼<rt>しつれい</rt></ruby>なことを<ruby>言<rt>い</rt></ruby>った。

    a. ばかり   b. ばかりに   c. あるばかり   d. あるばかりに

(7) Because his attempts at buttering the boss up were so obvious, he lost the boss's trust.

その<ruby>社員<rt>しゃいん</rt></ruby>はごますりが<ruby>露骨<rt>ろこつ</rt></ruby>な＿＿＿＿＿、<ruby>上司<rt>じょうし</rt></ruby>からの<ruby>信頼<rt>しんらい</rt></ruby>を<ruby>失<rt>うしな</rt></ruby>った。

    a. ばかり   b. ばかりに   c. とばかりに   d. ばかりに

(8) Kyle devoted himself to playing games, as if sleeping were a waste of time.

カイくんは<ruby>寝<rt>ね</rt></ruby>る<ruby>時間<rt>じかん</rt></ruby>ももったいない＿＿＿＿＿ゲームに<ruby>熱中<rt>ねっちゅう</rt></ruby>している。

    a. ばかり   b. ばかりに   c. とばかりに   d. ばかりに

III. 「～ばかりで（は）なく」 Not only ～, but ...

This expression is used to add more detail or information about something. It can be translated as "not only" or "in addition."

```
Noun
Verb
い-adjective
な-adjective ＋ な     ＋ ばかりで（は）なく
```

29. アジアやヨーロッパばかりではなく、彼女はアフリカにも行ったことがあります。

Not only has she been to Asia and Europe, she has also been to Africa.

30. 日本語ばかりでなく、中国語も話せるよ。

In addition to Japanese, I can also speak Chinese.

31. この町は静かなばかりではなく、町の人々はすごく優しい。

In addition to being a quiet/peaceful town, the people are also really nice.

32. 彼は本当に男前だ。そればかりではなく、運動神経も良い。
それで彼のことが好きな女性は多い。

He is really handsome. And not only that, he is also good at sports.
That's why there are so many girls that like him.

33. このパソコンは便利なばかりではなく、価格も安い。買った方がいいと思う。

Not only is this computer useful/convenient, the price is also cheap.
I think you should buy it.

IV. 「〜ばかりか」 In addition to 〜

This structure is essentially the exact same as what we saw above with 「〜ばかりで(は)なく」 in meaning and in structure.

```
Noun
Verb
い-adjective          ]  + ばかりか
な-adjective + な
```

34. <u>フランス語ばかりか</u>、彼女は英語もできる。
    In addition to French, she also speaks English.

35. 彼女は<u>可愛いばかりか</u>、頭もいいよ。
    Not only is she cute, she is also smart.

36. <u>品質が良くないばかりか</u>、値段も高い。誰も買わないでしょう。
    Not only is the quality bad, but the price is also expensive.
    Nobody is going to buy this, right?

37. 彼は漢字を<u>読めないばかりか</u>、ひらがなでも自分の名前さえ書けないよ。
    Not only can he not read Kanji, he can't even write his *own* name in Hiragana.

38. <u>肉ばかりか</u>、卵やチーズも食べない。
    In addition to meat, I don't eat eggs or cheese either.

単語を並び替えて、1つの文にしなさい。

Unscramble the following words to make sentences.

(9) Mom got angry at not only my little brother, but at me as well.

お母さん　弟　に　僕　ばかりでなく　怒られた　も

_____。

(10) Not only are "日" and "曰" easily confused, the number of strokes is also the same.

紛らわしい　と　画数　は　同じだ　ばかりではなく　「日」　も　「曰」

_____。

(11) He doesn't just say he'll do something, he actually does what he says.

ばかりでなく　行動　は　言う　も　する　彼

_____。

(12) Not only is Mr. Abe a good speaker, he is also a good listener.

上手な　聞き上手　阿部さん　が　話　は　でもある　ばかりではなく

_____。

(13) Not only did Mr. Nagano understand that difficult equation, but he was also able to apply it.

その難しい　理解する　応用する　方程式を　永野さんは　ばかりか
こともできる

_____。

(14) What's more, he was a terrible husband because not only did he cheat, but he also went into debt.

ばかりか　最低の　彼は　だった　なにより　浮気　借金もする　夫

_____。

(15) Not only was that older woman cheerful, she was also sophisticated.

上品な　おばあさんは　その　人　朗らかな　でもあった　ばかりか

_____。

Chapter 58
「～に加えて」 & 「～とともに」

I. 「～に加えて」 Not only ～, but ...

This next structure is used to add more information that is related to what has already been said. It's can be translated as "In addition," "What's more...", "Not only..., but..."

$$\boxed{\textbf{Noun} \ + \ \text{に加え(て)}}$$

1. 日本語に加えて、フランス語も出来る。
   I not only speak Japanese, but French as well.

2. 数学の宿題に加え、英語のもある。大変…。
   In addition to math homework, I also have English homework. Life is rough...

3. 買った株の価格が上がった。それに加え、ビットコインの価格も上がり続けている。
   お金持ちになるんだ！
   The price of the stock I bought went up. What's more, the price of Bitcoin keeps going up, too. I'm going to be rich!

4. 去年の夏休みはヨーロッパの色々な国に加えて、
   アフリカのあっちこっちにも行った。
   During last year's summer vacation, in addition to various countries in Europe, I also traveled around to difference places in Africa.

5. 日本って、津波に加えて、地震もよくある。やっぱり、ちょっと危ないね。
   In Japan, not only are there tsunamis, but there are quite a few earthquakes as well. Honestly, it's a little dangerous.

6. 頭がいいのに加えて、結構かっこいい。やっぱりモテモテだね。
   Not only is he smart, but he is also quite good looking. I bet he is popular with the ladies.

7. このあたりは静かなのに加えて、マンションの家賃も安い。
   In addition to being quiet/peaceful, the rent for apartments in this area is cheap.

8. たくさんの宿題があるのに加えて、明日の旅行の準備もしなきゃ。

Not only do I have a lot of homework, but I also need to get ready for tomorrow's trip.

To form this structure, we can only pair 「に加えて」 with nouns, but in example sentences 6 and 7, we have an い and a な-adjective (respectively). We can actually use any part-of-speech, as long as we nominalize it (that is "make it into a noun"). In this case, we are simply adding 「の」 to nominalize our two adjectives. We can also do the same for verbs, like in example sentence 8. We can also use 「こと」 for nominalization as well.

An easy way to remember the meaning of this structure is to keep in mind the meaning of the Kanji character 「加」 which actually means "addition" or "increase."

II. 「〜とともに」 Together; Along with 〜

This structure is very similar to 「一緒に」 and essentially means the same thing; "together." Also, please be sure to note that 「とともに」 can be written in Kanji as 「と共に」 and that you may see it written this way as well. The character 「共」 itself actually means "together," "with," or "alike."

Noun ＋ とともに

9. 休みの日、彼女とともにゆっくりしたいと思う。

On a day off, I want to spend a nice, relaxing day together with my girlfriend.

10. 友達と共に日本に行くことにした。

I decided to go to Japan along with my friend.

11. 今年、同級生とともに修学旅行に行きます。

I am going to go on a field trip with my class this year.

Another structure with 「〜とともに」 is used to express multiple events/actions happening at the same time. If it helps, you can also think of it as meaning two things happen "together."

> | **Noun that represents a change**
 Dictionary-form-verb | + とともに |

12. 人は年を取るとともに記憶力が低下していく。

As people get older, their memory (ability to remember) gets worse and worse.

13. ビットコインの価格が上がるとともに、買う人も増えた。

As the value of Bitcoin increases, the number of people buying it also went up.

14. 地球温暖化とともにシロクマの生息数が減りつつある。

Along with global warming, the polar bear population continues to decrease.

15. 円高とともに日本に来る観光客が少なくなっている。

As the value of the Japanese Yen increases, the number of tourists coming to Japan is becoming less and less.

16. 日本語が上手になると共に、友達が出来るのが楽になる。

As one's Japanese gets better, it becomes easier to make friends.

Some Guy's Pro-Tip

The word 「人口」 is translated as "population," but it can only be used to take about the population of people (as indicated by the character 「 人 」). In example sentence 14, to discuss the population of polar bears, we use the word 「生息」. 「生息」 is also used for plants/trees.

擬音語 Japanese Onomatopoeia – "Weather"

【ぽかぽか】　Warm and toasty; comfortable feeling
　　　　　　Ex. 今日はぽかぽか陽気だ。
　　　　　　Today is a bright and sunny day.

【むしむし】　To be humid
　　　　　　Ex. 日本の夏は湿気が高くてむしむしする。
　　　　　　Japan's summers are humid and muggy.

→Answer: P242

（　　　　　）内の単語を使って、1つの文を作りなさい。

Translate the following sentences into Japanese, using「に加え（て）」or「とともに」.

(1) Please add this cost on to the estimate.
（費用 / 見積もり / 加えて）

_____。

(2) We have hired more employees and further expanded our services.
（新しい社員 / 弊社 / 一層 / 拡充 / 加え）

_____。

(3) Mr. Nakamura always eats edamame with his beer.
（ビール / 枝豆 / とともに）

_____。

(4) Along with the aging society, the declining population is becoming more and more of a serious problem.
（高齢化 / 人口減少 / 深刻な / とともに）

_____。

(5) Along with reducing the weight of laptops, the engineers are also focusing on making them more energy efficient.
（技術者 / ノートパソコン / 軽量化 / 図る / 省電力化 / 注力 / とともに）

_____。

Chapter 59
「～として（は）」As a ～; For a ～

This next structure is used with nouns and is used to express, "As a [noun]..." or "For a [noun]..."

> **Noun ＋ として（は）**

1. 何年間もディスニーランドで働いているけど、<u>お客さんとして</u>行ったことはない。
   I have been working at Disneyland for a number of years, but I have never gone there as customer.

2. 彼はバスケットボールの<u>選手としては</u>背がちょっと低い。
   For a basketball player, he is a little on the shorter side.

3. <u>外国人としては</u>、彼の日本語のレベルは結構高いと思う。
   His Japanese level is quite high for a foreigner.

4. <u>人として</u>好きだけど、彼の音楽は好きじゃない。
   I like him as a person, but I don't like his music.

5. これは上司に<u>問題として</u>認められない。
   This will not be considered/seen as a problem by the boss.

6. その生徒は<u>好きな映画として</u>「となりのトトロ」をあげた。
   That student gave "Tonari no Totoro" as an example of a movie she liked.

→Answer: P242

単語（たんご）を並（なら）び替（か）えて、1つの文（ぶん）にしなさい。
Unscramble the following words to make sentences.

(1) Personally, I agree with her opinions.

彼女（かのじょ）　に　見解（けんかい）　一個人（いちこじん）としては　賛同（さんどう）する　の

_____。

(2) The reality is that fish consumption is increasing on a global scale.

世界的（せかいてき）　の　魚（さかな）　が　消費量（しょうひりょう）　増（ふ）えて　に　事実（じじつ）として　きている

_____。

(3) Until now, compulsory education has been accepted as a natural thing.

これまで　受（う）けてきた　を　当然（とうぜん）のこととして　義務教育（ぎむきょういく）

_____。

(4) Please think of that as never having happened.

なかったこと　は　として　考（かんが）えて　あの話（はなし）　ください

_____。

(5) Even those that are gifted are prone to making mistakes.

こともある　でも　時（とき）として　秀才（しゅうさい）　間違（まちが）える

_____。

Chapter 60
「～はもちろん ／ ～はもとより」
Let alone; Of course ～

This next structure is used to express that in addition to something else, another aspect of something is true. It is often translated as "also," "not to mention," or "let alone" to express something matter-of-factly.

The meaning of 「はもちろん」 and 「もとより」, when used this way, are the same. So, whichever one you use is simply based on your own personal preference.

Noun ＋ はもちろん ／ はもとより

---

1. 英語はもちろん、日本語もできるよ。
   Of course I speak English, but I can speak Japanese as well.

2. 教室の中では、食べ物はもとより水以外の飲み物もダメです。
   In class, of course food is not allowed, but any drink other than water is also prohibited.

3. 怪我した彼は走るのはもちろん、歩くこともできない。
   After hurting himself, he can't walk let alone run.

4. 運動が好きな彼は自分でサッカーするのはもちろん観るのも面白いと思っている。
   He likes sports. So, not only does he like to play soccer, he enjoys watching it too.

5. 国内はもとより、海外でも彼は結構愛されている。
   It goes without saying that domestically (in this country) he is well known,
   but he is quite well known abroad, as well.

6. 彼女はいい生徒です。
   自分の宿題はもとより、よく他の生徒も手伝ってあげるそうだ。
   She is a good student. Of course she does all of her homework, but she also helps other students with theirs.

191

7. ピクサーの映画って子供はもちろん、大人も楽しめる。

When it comes to Pixar movies, it goes without saying that children like them, but adults can enjoy them too.

8. あたなはもちろん、あなたの彼氏にもパーティーに来て欲しい。

Naturally I want you to come to the party, but I want your boyfriend to come as well.

9. 100キロはもとより、50キロでも持ち上げられないよ。

If I can't even lift 50 kilos, it stands to reason that I can't lift 100!

It is also worth mentioning that the word「もちろん」itself translates to "of course," and can be used as a word or expression on its own.

10.「手伝ってくれる？」「もちろん！」

"Well you help me?" "Of course!"

11.「あなた、日本語できる？」「もちろん、できるぞ！」

"You can speak Japanese?" "Of course I can!"

擬音語 Japanese Onomatopoeia – "Hair"

【さらさら】 Clean and dry hair
Ex. 彼女の長い髪の毛はさらさらで美しいね。
Isn't her long hair shiny and beautiful?

【ぼさぼさ】 Unkempt hair
Ex. 起きたばかりだから、髪の毛がぼさぼさしている。
I just woke up, so my hair is a mess.

【ふさふさ】 To have a lot of healthy hair
Ex. 私のおじいちゃんは90歳だけど、まだ髪の毛はふさふさしているよ。
My grandfather is 90 years old, but he still has a great head of hair.

【つるつる】 To have no hair
Ex. 彼はまだ20代なのに、もう頭がつるつるになっている。
He is still in his 20s, but he is already completely bald.

→Answer: P242

（　　　　）内の単語を使って、1つの文を作りなさい。

Translate the following sentences into Japanese, using 「はもとより」,「はもちろん」 or 「もちろん」.

(1) Not only does Jeremy speak Japanese, but he can speak English and Spanish as well.
（ジェレミー / はもとより）

_____。

(2) Of course, the mother not only shielded her child right away, but her dog as well.
（母親 / とっさに / ペットの犬 / はもちろん）

_____。

(3) It is unusually hot, so of course I have the AC turned on.
（異常な / クーラー / もちろん）

_____。

(4) This manufacturer's goods are first and foremost functional and safe as well.
（メーカー / 商品 / 機能性 / 安全性 / はもちろん）

_____。

(5) Sure enough, not only did he forget his plane ticket, but he forgot his passport as well.
（案の定 / 飛行機 / はもとより）

_____。

Chapter 61
「～をきっかけに / ～がきっかけで」
Explaining the reason for a change

This structure is used when we want to express how something was used as an opportunity to do something else, or to explain the reason for some change or development/advancement.

Noun + をきっかけに / にして / として / がきっかけで

1. 大学入学をきっかけに、ひとり暮らしを始めた。
   I started living by myself after starting college.

2. 結婚をきっかけにして、新しい家を買いました。
   Since I got married, I bought a new house.

3. 来年のオリンピックがきっかけで、たくさんの日本人は英語を勉強している。
   With the Olympics coming next year, many Japanese people are studying English.

4. 海外旅行がきっかけで、自国の文化について考えるようになりました。
   As a result of having traveled abroad, I started to think about my own country's culture.

5. アニメがきっかけで、日本の文化に興味を持つようになりました。
   With anime as a starting-off-point, I started to become interested in Japanese culture.

6. 日本人の彼女ができたのをきっかけに、日本語を勉強しだした。
   Considering I have a Japanese girlfriend, I started to study Japanese.

7. 友達に紹介されたことがきっかけとして、この本を読み始めた。*
   As a result of being recommended to me by a friend, I started to read this book.

8. 日本に行ったことがきっかけで、主人と知り合った。
   Going to Japan is what allowed me to meet my husband.

Some Guy's Pro-Tip

Please notice here in example sentence 7 that we have used 「こと」 to nominalize the phrase 「友達<ruby>友達<rt>ともだち</rt></ruby>に<ruby>紹介<rt>しょうかい</rt></ruby>された」. We do not have to only use single-words as nouns. 「の」 could have also been used for this purpose.

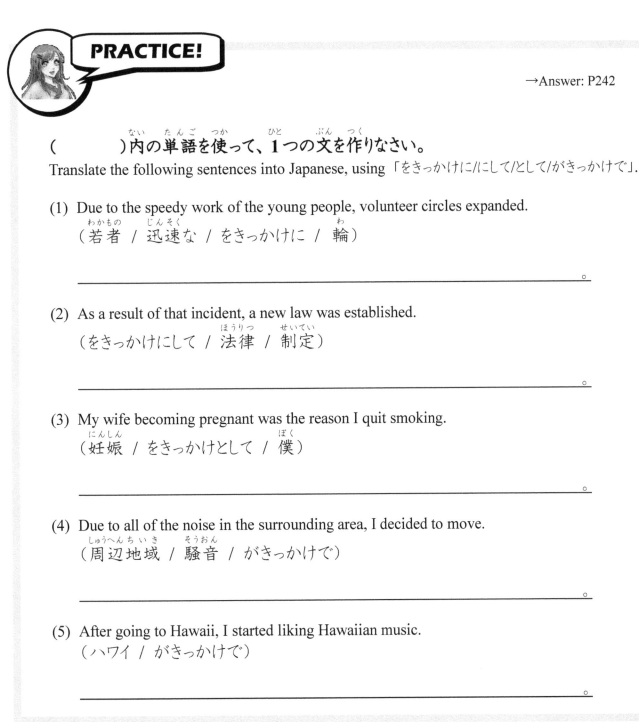

PRACTICE!

→Answer: P242

( )<ruby>内<rt>ない</rt></ruby>の<ruby>単語<rt>たんご</rt></ruby>を<ruby>使<rt>つか</rt></ruby>って、**1**つの<ruby>文<rt>ぶん</rt></ruby>を<ruby>作<rt>つく</rt></ruby>りなさい。

Translate the following sentences into Japanese, using 「をきっかけに/にして/として/がきっかけで」.

(1) Due to the speedy work of the young people, volunteer circles expanded.
(<ruby>若者<rt>わかもの</rt></ruby> / <ruby>迅速<rt>じんそく</rt></ruby>な / をきっかけに / <ruby>輪<rt>わ</rt></ruby>)

_____ 。

(2) As a result of that incident, a new law was established.
(をきっかけにして / <ruby>法律<rt>ほうりつ</rt></ruby> / <ruby>制定<rt>せいてい</rt></ruby>)

_____ 。

(3) My wife becoming pregnant was the reason I quit smoking.
(<ruby>妊娠<rt>にんしん</rt></ruby> / をきっかけとして / <ruby>僕<rt>ぼく</rt></ruby>)

_____ 。

(4) Due to all of the noise in the surrounding area, I decided to move.
(<ruby>周辺地域<rt>しゅうへんちいき</rt></ruby> / <ruby>騒音<rt>そうおん</rt></ruby> / がきっかけで)

_____ 。

(5) After going to Hawaii, I started liking Hawaiian music.
(ハワイ / がきっかけで)

_____ 。

Chapter 62
「べき」

I. 「〜べき」 Must 〜

This is a very useful suffix that expresses that something "must" be done, or that something is an obligation. We simply append it to a dictionary-form-verb to get "must verb." It has a similar usage to 「したほうがいい」 (should do something), but is considered to be a little "stronger" when telling someone to do something.

> **Dictionary-form-verb ＋ べき**

1. 日本語を話せるようになりたかったら、毎日勉強するべきだよ。*
   If you want to learn to speak Japanese, you must study every day

2. あんな失礼なことを言うなんて、先生に謝るべきだ。
   That you would say such a thing... you must apologize to your teacher.

3. あなたの彼氏はあまり優しくない。彼と別れるべきだと思う。
   Your boyfriend is not very nice. You ought to break up with him.

4. 寝る前に歯を磨くべきです。
   One must brush their teeth before going to bed.

5. あなたはもっと運動するべきです。
   You really ought to exercise more.

6. この映画はすっごく面白いよ！きみも絶対観るべきだ！*
   This movie is really good! You absolutely must see it!

7. 新車にするべきか中古を買うべきか迷っている。
   I am not sure whether I ought to be a new or a used car.

8. 試験に落ちた！もっと一生懸命勉強すべきだった…。
   I failed my test! I really ought to have studied harder...

You may also see 「するべき」 written as 「すべき」, but 「するべき」 is more conversational. You may even see it as 「すべし」 when you want to truly convey a strong feeling of obligation. As in...

Ex. オフィスに入る前にはノックすべし。

You should/must knock before coming into my office.

The character found in 「観る」 is read the exact same as 「見る」, and the meaning is also quite similar. They have the same meaning, but typically this character is used when you talk about watching television, or some kind of performance.

Ex. 彼女は今、歌舞伎を観ているところです。

She is currently watching Kabuki (a Kabuki performance).

II. 「Negating 〜べき」

How about if you want to tell someone that something must **_not_** be done? Well, that is pretty easy too. But we have to be careful. We do not conjugate the verb that we attach 「べき」 to. Instead, we simply append 「ではありません」 or other negative equivalents; じゃない、ではない、じゃありません _to_ 「べき」.

9. 先生にあんな失礼なことを言うべきではありません。

You mustn't say such rude things to your teacher.

10. 寝る前に飴を食べるべきじゃないよ。

You shouldn't/ought not to eat candy before going to bed.

11. あなたの彼氏はすごく優しい。彼と別れるべきじゃないと思う。

Your boyfriend is so nice. I don't think you ought to break up with him.

12. この映画はくだらない！観るべきじゃない。

This movie is awful. You definitely shouldn't see it.

13. 過去を忘れるべきではありません。

We mustn't forget the past.

14. カンニングを<u>するべきじゃない</u>。
   You must never cheat. (Cheating must be avoided)

15. 子供にアルコールを<u>売るべきじゃありません</u>！
   You absolutely must never sell alcohol to children!

16. あの試験は楽勝だった。あんなに<u>心配するべきじゃなかった</u>ね。
   That test was a breeze. I really didn't need to worry so much.

III. 「〜ざるべき」 Must not 〜

Some of you hard-core Japanese learners out there might be saying "Jeremy! That's not true. You can use 「べき」 with verbs conjugated to a negative-form!" Yes, yes, I know. And if this is you, congratulations! Your Japanese-skills are quite good.

Anyway, for those who are not aware, there is a somewhat classical style of Japanese that is negative and can take 「べき」. This book will not go into details about it, as it is a little beyond the scope of this book, but simply introduce some sentences using the 「ざる」 structure, which is made by just adding 「ざる」 to the ない-stem of the verb.

17. それは<u>言わざるべき</u>ことです。
   You mustn't say such a thing.

18. もう一杯ビールを<u>飲むべき</u>か、<u>飲まざるべき</u>か迷っている。
   I can't decide whether I should have another beer or not.

19. デザートを<u>食べるべき</u>か、<u>食べざるべき</u>か…ダイエット中だけど、
   美味しそうだから食べようかな。
   Should I have desert or not…I am on a diet, but it just looks so good that I have to have it.

「言わざるべき」 and 「言うべきではない」, for instance, have the same meaning, as do 「飲まざるべき」 and 「飲むべきではない」 or 「食べざるべき」 and 「食べるべきではない」. Today, however, you are not likely to hear anyone say the 「〜ざるべき」 structure because it is a style that is typically reserved for writing.

→Answer: P242

（　　　　）内の単語を使って、1つの文を作りなさい。

Translate the following sentences into Japanese, using「べき」or「ざるべき」

(1) Risk should be diversified.
（リスク / 分散 / べき）

_____。

(2) Even if you are dissatisfied, you mustn't resort to violence.
（不満 / 暴力 / 訴える / べき）

_____。

(3) He debated with himself whether or not to follow his angered girlfriend home.
（追う / 悩む / べき / ざるべき）

_____。

(4) Proceed with caution.
（注意 / すべし）

_____。

(5) You mustn't be absent from class without a reason.
（無断 / 欠席 / べき）

_____。

Chapter 63
「～ともなって/～ともない」&「<ruby>伴<rt>ともな</rt></ruby>う」

I. 「～ともなって / ～ともない」 Along with ～; At the same time as ～

The verb 「<ruby>伴<rt>ともな</rt></ruby>う」 by itself means "to accompany." This can help make understanding the meaning of this structure a little easier to understand and remember. We use 「～にともなって／～にともない」 to express that as one thing changes, another thing also changes as a result.

Noun Dictionary-form-verb	+ にともなって / にともない

1. <ruby>経営<rt>けいえい</rt></ruby>の<ruby>悪化<rt>あっか</rt></ruby>にともない、<ruby>多<rt>おお</rt></ruby>くの<ruby>社員<rt>しゃいん</rt></ruby>が<ruby>失業<rt>しつぎょう</rt></ruby>した。
   As business got worse, many employees lost their jobs.

2. <ruby>世界人口<rt>せかいじんこう</rt></ruby>が<ruby>増<rt>ふ</rt></ruby>えていくに<ruby>伴<rt>ともな</rt></ruby>い、いろいろな<ruby>問題<rt>もんだい</rt></ruby>が<ruby>起<rt>お</rt></ruby>こってきている。
   In conjunction with the increasing global population, many problems are occurring.

3. <ruby>日本語<rt>にほんご</rt></ruby>の<ruby>上達<rt>じょうたつ</rt></ruby>にともなって、<ruby>日本<rt>にほん</rt></ruby>の<ruby>生活<rt>せいかつ</rt></ruby>が<ruby>楽<rt>たの</rt></ruby>しくなる。
   As your Japanese improves, life in Japan becomes more enjoyable/fun.

4. ビットコインの<ruby>値段<rt>ねだん</rt></ruby>が<ruby>上<rt>あ</rt></ruby>がっている。
   それにともなって、ほかの<ruby>仮想通貨<rt>かそうつうか</rt></ruby>の<ruby>値段<rt>ねだん</rt></ruby>も<ruby>上<rt>あ</rt></ruby>がっている。
   The price of Bitcoin is rising.
   Along with that, other crypto-currencies' prices are also rising.

5. <ruby>工場<rt>こうじょう</rt></ruby>の<ruby>閉鎖<rt>へいさ</rt></ruby>にともなって、<ruby>周<rt>まわ</rt></ruby>りの<ruby>大気汚染<rt>たいきおせん</rt></ruby>が<ruby>改善<rt>かいぜん</rt></ruby>された。
   The local air pollution has gotten better since the factory closed down.

II. 「伴う」 To accompany

As mentioned above,「伴う」by itself can be used as a verb to describe that two things "go together" or "accompany each other."

6. 妻を伴って旅行に行きたいです。
   I'd like to go on a trip (together) with my wife.

7. 危険を伴う仕事だから、お給料は高いです。
   This job comes with dangerous risks, so the pay is high.

8. 自由にはそれに伴う責任があります。
   Being free comes with its own kind of responsibilities.

擬音語 (ぎおんご) Japanese Onomatopoeia – "Energetic/Vivacious"

【わくわく】 Wanting to dance from happiness or anticipation
Ex. 子供達は、わくわくしながらクリスマスプレゼントを開けた。
The children excitedly opened their Christmas presents.

【うきうき】 Ex. 彼はうきうきしながらデートに出かけた。
He left for his date with a spring in his step.

【いきいき】 To be energetic and vivacious
Ex. この島の人たちは、みんないきいきしているね。
The people on this island are healthy and vivacious.

【のびのび】 Living freely and carefree
Ex. つまらない仕事を辞めて、のびのびと生活することにした。
I decided to quit my boring job and live a life of leisure.

【るんるん】 To be in a great mood; ecstatic
Ex. 今日はいいことがあったから、るんるん気分だ！
Something good happened today and I am on top of the world.

【ぴんぴん】 Being healthy and energetic
Ex.「おばあさんはお元気ですか？」「はい、とてもぴんぴんしています。」
"Is your grandmother well?" "Yes, she is full of vim and vinegar."

【すくすく】 To develop healthily and well
Ex. その子猫はすくすくと大きくなった。
That kitten grew up (got big) fast.

→Answer: P243

PRACTICE!

「にともなって」、「にともない」、「伴う」を使って、2つの文を1つの文にしなさい。

Take the following sentences and combine them into one, using 「にともなって」、「にともない」、or 「伴う」.

(1) 地震の発生。広い地域で停電が起こった。(にともない)

Along with the earthquake, there were widespread blackouts.

_____。

(2) オリンピックの開催。街のインフラが整ってきた。(にともなって)

Because of the Olympics, the infrastructure of the city has been improved.

_____。

(3) 日が沈む。だんだん赤焼け空になってきた。(にともない)

As the sun went down, the sky turned red.

_____。

(4) 台風の勢力が強まる。風が強くなってきた。(にともなって)

As the force of the typhoon grew, the wind became stronger.

_____。

(5) 出産のときの陣痛。かなりの痛み。(伴う)

With childbirth comes great pain.

_____。

Chapter 64
はんめん
「〜半面」
On the other hand, despite 〜

This is a structure that essentially translates to "despite...," "although..." or, "on the other hand."

In fact, an easy way to remember this structure is that the character 「半」 in 「半面」 means "half." The character 「面」 means "face" or "side." So, put them together and you get "half of a side." Keeping this in mind, we can more easily understand its meaning in pointing out one point-of-view or "side" of some topic to compare it to another.

Noun + である	
Verb	+ 半面
い-adjective	
な-adjective + な	

1. 携帯電話は便利な半面、トラブルも多い。
   Although cell-phones are convenient, they also cause a lot of trouble/problems.

2. 僕はスポーツが得意な半面、勉強は全然だめだ。
   Despite being good at sports, I am a rather poor student.

3. このブランドは高い半面、とても丈夫で長持ちする。
   Although this brand is expensive, it is well made and will last a long time.

4. この薬はよく効く半面、副作用もひどいらしい。
   On one hand, this medicine is really effective. On the other, its side-effects are quite severe.

5. スミスさんは外国人である半面、日本語はとても上手だ。
   Even though Mr. Smith is a foreigner, his Japanese is really good.

6. アリゾナの夏は暑い半面、湿気がほとんどない。
   Although summers in Arizona are hot, there is very little humidity.

7. 子供である半面、とても賢い。
   Despite being a child, he is quite clever.

「半面」を使って、2つの文を1つの文にしなさい。

Take the following sentences and combine them into one, using 「半面」.

(1) 彼は厳しい上司です。彼は頼れる指導者です。

He is a tough boss, but, on the other hand, he is a reliable leader.

_____。

(2) ペンギンは飛翔能力が退化した。ペンギンは泳ぐ能力が備わった。

While penguins lost the ability to fly, they are equipped with the ability to swim.

_____。

(3) 生意気な子供は憎たらしい。生意気な子供は愛おしい。

I don't like bratty children, but I still think they are adorable.

_____。

(4) トライアスロンは過酷。トライアスロンはゴールした時の達成感が大きい。

On one hand, triathlons are brutal. On the other, when you reach the goal, you feel a great sense of accomplishment.

_____。

Chapter 65
「～ついでに」
While you're at it; Taking the opportunity

This structure is used when we want to express that we will take advantage of some situation to do another thing. That may be a little confusing, but if you read the example sentences below, I promise it will make more sense. It can be translated as "to take advantage of...", "while you are at it..." or "taking the opportunity..."

It may also be worth noting that the Kanji form is written as 「序（ついで）に」, but you will a typically see it written out in Hiragana.

> **Noun + の**
> **Dictionary-form-verb**
> **Casual-past-tense-form verb casual** } + ついでに

1. スーパーに行（い）ったついでに、銀行（ぎんこう）にも行（い）ってきた。
   I stopped by the bank after I going to the store.

2. 郵便局（ゆうびんきょく）に行（い）くついでに、この本（ほん）を図書館（としょかん）に返（かえ）してくれる？
   On your way to the post office, could you return this book to the library for me?

3. 先週（せんしゅう）、出張（しゅっちょう）で東京（とうきょう）に行（い）った。ついでに友達（ともだち）とロボットレストランに行（い）った。
   やっぱり面白（おもしろ）かった！*
   I went to Tokyo last week on a business trip. Since I was there, I met up with a friend and we went to the Robot Restaurant. As expected, it was awesome!

4. お母（かあ）さんは犬（いぬ）を散歩（さんぽ）させたついでに、今夜（こんや）の晩（ばん）ご飯（はん）を買（か）ってきた。
   While Mom was walking the dog, she bought tonight's dinner.

5. もう出（で）かけるの？じゃぁ、それならついでにゴミを出（だ）してきてくれる？
   Are you leaving already? In that case, would you mind throwing this trash out for me on your way out?

6. 今（いま）から田中部長（たなかぶちょう）のオフィスに行（い）きますか？
   だったら、ついでにこれを彼（かれ）に渡（わた）してくれますか？
   Are you going to Mr. Tanaka's office now?
   If so, would you mind giving this to him for me?

Some Guy's Pro-Tip

If you have some free time, Google "Robot Restaurant." It's not really a restaurant, but more of a show with "Robots." I had the opportunity to go there myself and had a great time. If you ever make it out to Tokyo, I recommend checking it out.

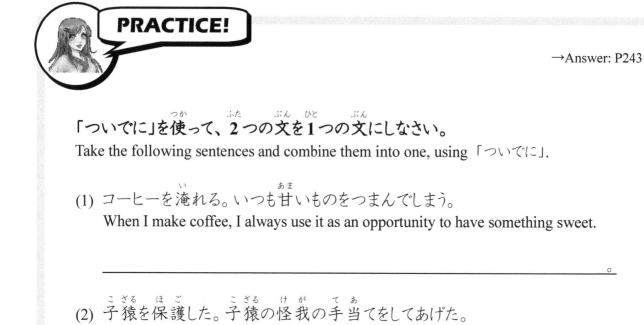

PRACTICE!

→Answer: P243

「ついでに」を使って、2つの文を1つの文にしなさい。

Take the following sentences and combine them into one, using 「ついでに」.

(1) コーヒーを淹れる。いつも甘いものをつまんでしまう。

When I make coffee, I always use it as an opportunity to have something sweet.

_____。

(2) 子猿を保護した。子猿の怪我の手当てをしてあげた。

While I was looking after the baby monkey, I treated its injury.

_____。

(3) 話。離婚の手続きについて相談してみた。

Since we were on the subject, I also asked about divorce proceedings.

_____。

(4) 引っ越す。家具を全て新調することにした。

I used the fact that we were moving as an opportunity to get all new furniture.

_____。

(5) 出張で福岡に行った。おばさんに会いに行った。

Since I went to Fukuoka, I took it as an opportunity to meet with my aunt.

_____。

206

Chapter 66
「～くせに」
Even though; And yet

This next structure is *extremely* useful for daily conversation, so be sure to study this lesson multiple times. It essentially means "even though" or "despite (the fact that)" and is most often used when teasing someone, but it can also be used in a more serious tone to criticize or accuse someone as well. So, this one has a bit of range.

You may also note that it is quite similar in meaning to 「のに」, but 「くせに」 carries a bit of a stronger tone and has a more negative "impact." So, even though it is often used when joking around with friends, you have to be careful when using it because you might inadvertently offend someone.

> **Noun ＋ の**
> **Casual-form-verb**
> **い-adjective**
> **な-adjective ＋ な**
> ＋ くせに

1. 彼女は８年間日本に<u>住んでいたくせに</u>、日本語は<u>全く</u>できない。
   Even though she lived in Japan for eight years, she can't speak Japanese *at all*.

2. 「この漢字、全然読めない。」「<u>日本人のくせに</u>…。」
   "I can't read this Kanji at all." "You call yourself Japanese..."

3. <u>暑がりのくせに</u>、なんでマフラーを<u>巻</u>いているの？
   You always complain about it being hot, so why are you wearing a scarf?

4. 背が<u>高いくせに</u>、バスケは<u>下手</u>だね。
   Despite being tall, you're not very good at basketball, are you?

5. <u>アメリカ人のくせに</u>、今の大統領が誰か本当に知らないの？
   You call yourself an American and yet you don't even know who the current president is?

6. また彼女が僕の名前を忘れた。何回も<u>聞いたくせに</u>。
   She forgot my name again, even though she's asked several times already.

7. 寒がっているくせにアイスが食べたいなんて…。

   You are complaining about being cold, yet you want to eat ice cream…

8. あなたは彼のことが大嫌いなくせに、なんで助けてやるの？

   Even though you despise him, why are you going to help him?

9. 下手なくせに、うちのお母さんはカラオケが大好きです。

   Even though she is terrible at it, my mother loves to sing karaoke.

擬音語 Japanese Onomatopoeia – "Uneasy/Fear"

【どきどき】
The state of your heart beating faster because of exercise, excitement, anxiety, fear, or expectation.
Ex. 明日のスピーチの事を考えると、どきどきする

When I think about the speech I have to give tomorrow, my heart starts beating faster/beating out of my chest.

【はらはら】
Expressing concern over the outcome or consequence of some action or event
Ex. はらはらしながら、ボクシングの試合を観ていた。

I was watching the boxing match with trepidation. / I was on pins-and-needles during the boxing match.

【ぶるぶる】
One's body shaking from cold or fear
Ex. 雷に驚いた子犬はぶるぶる震えていた。

The puppy was shaking in fright after being scared by the thunder.

【びくびく】
To feel scared or uneasy
Ex. 彼らはお化け屋敷にびくびくしながら入っていった。

They entered the haunted house with trepidation.

【ひやひや】
Can't be calm due to worry or fear
Ex. ホラー映画をひやひやしながら観た。

I nervously/anxiously watched the horror movie.

【そわそわ】
Feeling nervous or restless; fidgety
Ex. 入学試験の結果をそわそわしながら待った。

I was anxious as I held the results of my entrance exams.

【たじたじ】
To be overwhelmed and have a reaction
Ex. 彼女は本物の虎を見て、たじたじとなった。

She saw an actual tiger and became really excited.

→Answer: P243

<ruby>単語<rt>たんご</rt></ruby>を<ruby>並<rt>なら</rt></ruby>び<ruby>替<rt>か</rt></ruby>えて、1つの<ruby>文<rt>ぶん</rt></ruby>にしなさい。

Unscramble the following words to make sentences.

(1) Even though you are a fisherman you hate fish-based dishes? That's weird.

くせに　<ruby>魚料理<rt>さかなりょうり</rt></ruby>　の　<ruby>変<rt>へん</rt></ruby>なの　<ruby>漁師<rt>りょうし</rt></ruby>　だなんて　<ruby>嫌<rt>きら</rt></ruby>い　が

_____。

(2) You don't know anything, so don't talk as if you do!

<ruby>知<rt>し</rt></ruby>った　<ruby>口<rt>くち</rt></ruby>　<ruby>何<rt>なに</rt></ruby>も　<ruby>利<rt>き</rt></ruby>かないで　ような　くせに　<ruby>知<rt>し</rt></ruby>らない　を

_____！

(3) I can see that really you are lonely, and that you are only putting on a front.

<ruby>心細<rt>こころぼそ</rt></ruby>い　は　<ruby>強<rt>つよ</rt></ruby>がっちゃって　<ruby>本当<rt>ほんとう</rt></ruby>　くせに

_____。

(4) Even though you are a man, you cry. How pathetic.

<ruby>泣<rt>な</rt></ruby>く　の　<ruby>情<rt>なさ</rt></ruby>けないね　なんて　<ruby>男<rt>おとこ</rt></ruby>　で　くせに　<ruby>人前<rt>ひとまえ</rt></ruby>

_____。

(5) Even though that kid is a coward, he still wants to go into the haunted house.

<ruby>臆病<rt>おくびょう</rt></ruby>な　その<ruby>子供<rt>こども</rt></ruby>　お<ruby>化<rt>ば</rt></ruby>け<ruby>屋敷<rt>やしき</rt></ruby>　は　<ruby>入<rt>はい</rt></ruby>りたがる　くせに　に

_____。

(6) You're tired, so why don't you say no to your friend's invitation?

<ruby>友達<rt>ともだち</rt></ruby>　<ruby>誘<rt>さそ</rt></ruby>い　を　<ruby>疲<rt>つか</rt></ruby>れている　<ruby>断<rt>ことわ</rt></ruby>らないの　くせに　どうして　からの

_____？

Chapter 67
「～っぱなし」
Leaving something on or as it is

We can use 「～っぱなし」 with the ます-stem of a verb to express that something has been left in a certain state or condition for a period of time; like maybe you went to bed and left the television on or you left the house and left the water in the faucet running. As such, it is often used to describe something that was done by accident.

ます-stem ＋ っぱなし

---

1. おもちゃを<u>出しっぱなし</u>にしないで！ちゃんと片付けなさい！
   Don't just leave your toys all over the place! Clean them up!

2. 疲れている…。今日はずっと<u>立ちっぱなし</u>で働いていた。座りたい。
   I'm beat... I was standing all day at work. I just want to sit down.

3. 昨日の夜、エアコンを<u>つけっぱなし</u>で寝たから風邪をひいてしまった。
   I fell asleep last night with the A.C. on and ended up catching a cold.

4. 窓を<u>開けっぱなし</u>で家を出た。危なかった…。
   I went out with my windows left wide-open. That could have been bad...

5. あそこにずっと<u>泣きっぱなし</u>の子供がいる。迷子かな…。
   There is a kid over there that just keeps crying. I wonder if he's lost...

6. 歯を磨きながら、水を<u>出しっぱなし</u>にするな。
   Don't leave the water running while brushing your teeth.

7. 店の前にたくさんの傘が<u>置きっぱなし</u>になっている。
   There are a ton of forgotten umbrellas in front of the store.

最も適切なものを1つ選びなさい。

Choose the right "っぱなし-phrase" to fill in the blanks.

(1) My wife always goes out with the housework half-finished.
　　妻はいつも家事を＿＿＿＿＿＿＿＿にして出かける。

　　　a. やるっぱなし　　b. やりっぱなし　　c. したっぱなし　　d. するっぱなし

(2) Since running a television advertisement, that restaurant's phone has been ringing off the hook for reservations.
　　そのレストランはテレビで紹介されてから予約の電話が＿＿＿＿＿＿＿＿になった。

　　　a. 鳴りっぱなし　　b. 鳴るっぱなし　　c. かけるっぱなし　　d. かかりっぱなし

(3) He has an open personality.
　　彼は＿＿＿＿＿＿＿＿な性格だ。

　　　a. 開きっぱなし　　b. 開くっぱなし　　c. 開けっぱなし　　d. 開けっぱなし

(4) I am looking forward to hitting some balls at the driving range this weekend.
　　週末にゴルフの＿＿＿＿＿＿＿＿に行くのが楽しみだ。

　　　a. 叩きっぱなし　　b. 練習しっぱなし　　c. しっぱなし　　d. 打ちっぱなし

(5) The newly-wed woman wouldn't stop talking about how wonderful married life is.
　　新婚の彼女は終始＿＿＿＿＿＿＿＿だった。

　　　a. 話しっぱなし　　b. 聞きっぱなし　　c. のろけっぱなし　　d. なりっぱなし

Chapter 68
「～きれない」&「～きる」
Cannot finish, cannot ～; To complete ～

First, we'll take a look at using 「～きれない」. This structure is used when we want to express that something cannot be done or finished to completion, perhaps because it is too hard or there is just too much of something. We'll take a look at some example sentences below to help make it a little easier to understand. But first, let's see how we form this structure.

It is also worth noting that in Kanji form it is written as 「切_きれない」.

> ます-stem-verb ＋ きれない

1. ご飯_{はん}の量_{りょう}が多_{おお}くて僕_{ぼく}は一人_{ひとり}でこれを<u>食_たべきれない</u>。一緒_{いっしょ}に食_たべる？
   This portion is quite large and I can't eat it all by myself. Would you join me?

2. 時間_{じかん}があんまりないから、今日_{きょう}の宿題_{しゅくだい}を<u>やりきれなさそう</u>。手伝_{てつだ}ってくれる？
   I don't have much time, and it doesn't seem like I'll be able to finish my homework. Can you help me?

3. 1日_{いちにち}ではThe Lord of the Rings_{ザ ロード オブ ザ リング}を<u>読_よみ切_きれない</u>。絶対_{ぜったい}に。
   There is absolutely *no way* you can read through The Lord of the Rings in a single day.

4. 彼女_{かのじょ}はすごいお金_{かね}持_もちだよ。<u>使_{つか}いきれない</u>ほどお金_{かね}を持_もっている。
   She is extremely rich, man. She couldn't spend it all if she tried.

5. 彼女_{かのじょ}は怒_{いか}りを<u>抑_{おさ}えきれず</u>に彼氏_{かれし}に怒鳴_{どな}った。
   Unable to suppress her anger, she screamed and yelled at her boyfriend.

6. その理論_{りろん}を<u>理解_{りかい}しきれない</u>。
   I cannot completely understand that theory.

7. 昨日_{きのう}は全然元気_{ぜんぜんげんき}じゃなかったからフルマラソンを<u>走_{はし}り切_きれなかった</u>。
   I didn't feel well at all yesterday, so I wasn't able to complete the full marathon.

8. 彼_{かれ}のこと<u>諦_{あきら}めきれない</u>…。
   I cannot give up (forget about) him...

Please also notice that 「切れる」 can be conjugated as a normal Type I verb. In example sentence 2, we changed it to 「切れなさそう」. In example sentence 5, we changed it to 「切れずに」, and in example sentence 6, we conjugated it to the past-tense; 「切れなかった」.

We can also use 「きれる」 with the verb 「待つ」 (to wait) to express anticipation, or that we "can't wait" for something.

9. 夏休みが<u>待ちきれない</u>！どこかに旅行したいな。
   I can't wait for summer vacation. I want to travel somewhere.

10. 子供たちは明日の朝まで<u>待ちきれなさそう</u>な顔をしている。
    今、クリスマスプレゼントを開けたいって。
    The kids' expressions seem to say that they can't wait for tomorrow.
    They say they want to open their Christmas presents now.

11. 次のワンピースの単行本が出るのが<u>待ちきれない</u>！早く読みたい！
    I can't wait for the next One Piece book to come out! I want to read it now!

12. すごく腹減ってる。ご飯が<u>待ちきれない</u>。
    I'm so hungry. I might not make it to lunch...

Now let's take a more in-depth look at using 「きる」. We use this structure when we want to express that we have successfully completed something and feel a sense of satisfaction in having done so, or to express that we do something "completely" or "to our utmost."

13. すごいでしょう！俺一人で3つのコース料理を<u>食べ切った</u>。お腹一杯…。
    Amazing, right? I ate a whole three-course meal by myself. Now I'm full.

14. 1日でこの本を<u>読み切った</u>。面白かった。
    I read this whole book in a single day. It was really interesting.

15. 私は彼を<u>信じ切っている</u>から、何でもサポートします。
    I have complete faith in him, so I support him in whatever he does.

16. 水ある？のどが<u>乾ききっている</u>。
    Is there any water? My throat is absolutely parched.

17. 今日一日中働いていたから、もう疲れ切ってしまった。
   I worked all day, so I'm dead tired.

18. ちょっと1000円貸してくれる？もう自分のお金を使い切ったから。
   Could you possibly loan me 1,000 Yen? I have already used up all of my money.

19. UFOは存在しているとなぜ言い切れるの？証拠は？
   How can you say that UFO's exist? Where is your proof?

擬音語 Japanese Onomatopoeia – "Anger"

【いらいら】 When something doesn't go how you want it to and you feel strung out.
   Ex. 彼は渋滞にはまると、いつもいらいらする。
      Whenever he gets stuck in jam, he gets angry/annoyed.

【むかむか】 Feeling anger from the depths of your soul.
   Ex. 彼女の身勝手に、むかむかする。
      Her self-centered attitude makes me furious.

【かりかり】 Quick to anger. Likely to fly off the handle
   Ex. 今、上司はかりかりしているから、あまり話しかけないでおこう。
      Right now, the boss is in one of his moods, so I think I'll not talk with him.

【かんかん】 To be steaming mad
   Ex. 彼は大事にしてたゲーム機を壊されてかんかんに怒っている。
      His beloved gaming console was broken and he was flipping out.

【ぷりぷり】 To get mad and be in a bad mood
   Ex. 彼女はぷりぷりしながら部屋を出て行った。
      She left the room in a huff.

【ぴりぴり】 Someone/Something is angry or in a bad mood, the atmosphere is bad
   Ex. お父さんがお母さんを怒らせたから、今日の夕食はぴりぴりしてた。
      Dad upset Mom, so tonight's dinner was rather uncomfortable.

最も適切なものを1つ選びなさい。

Choose the right "きれない/きる-phrase" to fill in the blanks.

(1) I saw that movie more times than I can count.

その映画を数え_____くらい何度も観ました。

a. きる   b. きれない   c. きれる   d. ることができる

(2) The corrupt politicians went down one after the other.

腐敗_____政治家たちは次々と失脚していった。

a. しきれない   b. しきる   c. しきった   d. しきれる

(3) I am absolutely exhausted.

くたくたに疲れ_____いる。

a. きって   b. きった   c. きれない   d. きれないで

(4) Mom made a feast that it doesn't look like we'll be able to finish.

お母さんは食べ_____量のご馳走を作った。

a. きれる   b. きれない   c. きる   d. きれなさそうな

(5) From now on, I won't have anything to do with you!

もうこれ以上あなたのことは面倒_____よ！

a. 見きれない   b. 見きれる   c. 見きる   d. 見れる

Chapter 69
「〜ずに」 & 「〜ずにはいられない」

I. 「〜ずに」 Without 〜

This next structure is paired with the ない-stem of a verb to express "without [verb]ing."

By this point in your Japanese learning career, you should already be familiar with how to conjugate a verb to the ない-form. If you need a little bit of a review, you can check out Chapter 12 of my first book. If you can comfortably conjugate to the ない-form of a verb, however, using this structure will be a breeze.

All we are doing is appending 「ずに」 to the verb's ない-stem. This works for all Type I and Type II verbs. This also works for the Type III verb 「来る」, but we will see a little bit below that 「する」 has a special conjugation with this structure.

Verb's ない-stem + ずに

1. うっかりドアに鍵をかけずに家を出てしまった。
   I left my house without locking the door by mistake.

2. 彼は約束の時間には来ず、結局私は３０分も待たされた。
   He didn't come at our scheduled time, and I had to wait 30 minutes.

3. 彼女は何も言わずに急に泣き出した。
   Without saying a word, she suddenly began to cry.

4. 今朝コーヒーを飲まずに会社に来たから、今日はちょっと眠いな。
   気合いを入れないと。
   I came to the office without having any coffee this morning, so I'm a little tired today.
   I need to do something to wake up.

5. 辞書を引かずにこの手紙を書いたんだけど、
   間違いがないかチェックしてもらえる？
   I wrote this letter without using a dictionary.
   Could you check to see if there are any mistakes?

6. 私があなたに言ったことを忘れずにね。
   Don't forget what I told you.

7. 会社から何も伝えられずにクビになってしまった。
   I was fired from my company without being told anything.

Of course, the ない-form of「する」is「しない」but we don't say「しせず」. The verb「する」, as per usual, behaves a little differently than other verbs and has somewhat of an irregular formation. The「ずに」form of「する」is「せずに」.

8. 勉強せずに試験に受かるわけないだろう。
   There is no way you can pass the test without studying.

9. 練習せずに上手になるなんて無理でしょう。
   It is impossible to get good at something without practicing.

10. 田中さんは挨拶せずにそのままオフィスに入った。何かあったかな…。
    Mr. Tanaka just went into his office without greeting anyone.
    I wonder if something happened...

Some Guy's Pro-Tip

There are ずに-forms of the verbs「ある」/「有る」and「いる」/「居る」, which are「有らず」and「居ず」, but they are typically reserved for classical Japanese, and you are not likely to encounter them in regular, day-to-day life.

II. 「～ずにはいられない」 Cannot help but ～

Building off of what we just learned with 「～ずに」, this is another useful grammar structure that express you "cannot help but [verb]."

The formation is exactly the same as above, but instead of 「ずに」 we are appending 「ずにはいられない」 to our verb's ない-stem.

> **Verb's ない-stem ＋ ずにはいられない**

11. これは<u>泣かずにはいられない</u>小説です。ぜひ読んでみてください。
   This novel will definitely make you cry. Please give it a read.

12. 私はお酒を<u>飲まずにはいられない</u>。特に梅酒が好き。飲んだことある？
   I just have to have alcohol. I especially like plum wine. Have you ever had it before?

13. 彼女に嫌われているのに、彼女に<u>電話せずにはいられなかった</u>。
   もちろん、彼女は出なかった。
   She hates me (I am hated by her), but I still couldn't help calling her.
   Of course, she didn't pick up.

14. 彼は彼女のことを<u>考えずにはいられない</u>。
   He can't help but think about her.

15. 彼を見て<u>叫ばずにはいられなかった</u>。
   I saw him and I couldn't help but call to him.

→Answer: P243

単語を並び替えて、1つの文にしなさい。

Unscramble the following words to make sentences.

(1) Mrs. Yoshida, without the help of her parents, put herself through college.

吉田さん　大学の学費　親に　を　頼ら　払った　ずに　は　自分で

_____。

(2) That shogi player, even when playing against children, shows no mercy.

でも　せずに　その棋士　手加減　は　指した　子供相手　将棋を

_____。

(3) I can't help but be amazed by his stupid mistake.

いられない　呆れ　彼の　失敗に　ずには　間抜けな

_____。

(4) She bungee-jumped without any hesitation whatsoever.

バンジージャンプ　は　彼女　を　飛んだ　ずに　ためらわ

_____。

(5) I can't help but feel sympathetic toward that person's background.

同情　生い立ち　せずには　には　あの人　の　いられない

_____。

Chapter 70
「〜たて」 Just finished; Fresh

This next structure is attached to the ます-stem of verbs to express that something was *just* finished or that something is "fresh." This is a structure you will often see used to describe food. Please also note that the Kanji-form of this structure is written as 「立て」.

ます-stem ＋ たて

---

1. このパンは焼きたてです。
   This is freshly baked bread.

2. 天ぷらは揚げたてが一番おいしい。食べてみてください。
   Just-fried tempura is the most delicious. Please try some.

3. このノートに書いてあるフレーズは覚えたてです。後で復習します。
   I just learned the phrases written in this notebook. Later, I'm going to review them.

A more common use of this structure, though, is to also append 「の」 to 「たて」 and turn our verb into an adjective.

---

4. やっぱり、焼きたてのパンは美味しくてたまらない。
   Yeah, bread that is fresh out of the oven tastes like heaven.

5. 学びたての単語をノートに書いておいてください。
   Please be sure to write newly learned words down in your notebook.

6. できたてのたい焼きは熱いので火傷しないようにしてください。
   Freshly baked *taiyaki* is hot, be careful not to burn yourself.

7. 淹れたてのコーヒーの香りは最高ですね。
   The smell of fresh brewed coffee is the beset.

8. このお寿司屋さんは捕れたての魚しか使わないから、
全ての料理はとても新鮮で美味しいです。
This sushi shop only uses freshly caught fish, so all of the dishes are fresh and delicious.

PRACTICE!

→Answer: P243

（　　　）内の単語を使って、1つの文を作りなさい。
Translate the following sentences into Japanese, using 「たて」.

(1) That wall was freshly painted, so be careful.
（壁 / ペンキ / 塗る）

_____ 。

(2) This guide book is extremely useful for people who just came to Japan.
（来る / ガイドブック / 役に立つ）

_____ 。

(3) You can buy freshly-picked vegetables at the farmer's market.
（ファーマーズマーケット / 採れる）

_____ 。

(4) Whenever I work at my uncle's orchard, I can eat freshly-picked apples.
（農園 / もぎる）

_____ 。

(5) When I first got married, I wasn't a very good cook.
（結婚する / 料理 / あまり）

_____ 。

Chapter 71
「〜さえ」 & 「〜すら」

I. 「〜さえ」 Even 〜

「〜さえ」 is often translated into English as "even." We use it to express surprise or emphasize some salient point, as in "Even I can do that," or "I don't have time to even brush my teeth!"

> **Noun**
> **て-form-verb**　　　 + さえ
> **ます-form-verb**

1. 最近、仕事が忙しくて、昼ご飯を食べる<u>時間さえ</u>ないんだ。
   Lately, work has been so busy that I don't even have time to eat lunch.

2. <u>子供でさえ</u>この漢字を読めるよ。
   Even kids can read this Kanji character, man.

3. 簡単な<u>文章でさえ</u>も分かりません。
   I can't even understand simple sentences.

4. 彼女は<u>親にさえ</u>相談せずに彼と結婚した。
   She married him without even consulting her parents first.

5. 彼は何年も日本に住んでいるのに、カタカナで自分の<u>名前さえ</u>
   書けないらしい。
   He has been living in Japan for several years, but I heard that he can't even use Katakana to write his own name.

6. 彼女は僕からの手紙を<u>読むことさえ</u>せずに、ゴミ箱に放り投げた。
   She tossed the letter I wrote to her in the garbage without even reading it.

7. いくら頼んでも山中さんは<u>私と会ってさえ</u>くれなかった。
   No matter how many times I asked, Mr. Yamanaka refused to even meet with me.

8. 頭が良い<u>太郎君でさえ</u>もこの問題はできなかった。やっぱり、難しいね。
   Even Taro the brainiac couldn't do this problem. That means it must be hard.

Using this structure with nominalized verbs is also quite common. If you remember from before, we can nominalize a verb by simply appending 「の」 or 「こと」 and then treat the verb or verb-phrase as a regular noun like in example sentence 6 above. Here are a few more examples.

9. 僕は自分の名前を書くことさえできない。
I can't even write my own name.

10. 彼女と連絡を取っていません。今、どこに住んでいるのかさえ知りません。
I don't keep in touch with her. I don't even know where she is living now.

11. このロボットは飛ぶことさえできるぞ。すごいでしょう。
This robot can even fly. Amazing, right?

You may have noticed that some sentences included some extra particles like 「で」 and 「も」. These are simply added for extra emphasis.

12. 子供さえできるよ。
Even kids can do it.

13. 子供でさえできるよ。
Even kids can do it.

14. 子供でさえもできるよ。
Even kids can do it.

All of these sentences have the same meaning, "Even a child can do it," but the degree of emphasis increases a bit with 「でさえ」 and increases even more with 「でさえも」.

Other sentences, like example sentence 4 above, even use other particles like 「に」. Don't let this confuse you. Remember, the point of using 「さえ」 is to add emphasis. Example sentence 4 would make perfect sense without 「さえ」 and would simply read as:

Ex. 彼女は親に相談せずに彼と結婚した。
Without consulting her parents, she married him.

But with 「さえ」 we get:

Ex. 彼女は親にさえ相談せずに彼と結婚した。
Without even consulting her parents, she married him.

Though the difference is subtle, it is clear that the speaker wants to express their surprise or astonishment at how she didn't even talk about it with her parents before "marrying him."

（　　　　）内の単語を使って、1つの文を作りなさい。

Translate the following sentences into Japanese, using 「さえ」.

(1) If only I had money, I would head to Hawaii straight away.
（お金 / ハワイ）

_____。

(2) As long as I go on living, we will be able to meet some time.
（生きる / 会える）

_____。

(3) I hear that AI is even able to learn.
（人工知能（ＡＩ） / 学習）

_____。

(4) I was even studying Japanese in my dreams.
（夢の中 / 勉強）

_____。

(5) This problem is so simple that even I can understand it.
（問題 / 簡単）

_____。

II. 「〜すら」 Even 〜

> **Noun ＋ すら / ですら / にすら**

1. 今朝、僕は忙しくて歯を磨く時間すらなかった。
   I was so busy this morning that I didn't even have time to brush my teeth.

2. 日本人ですら、この漢字を読めない。
   Even Japanese people can't read this Kanji character.

3. この問題は友達にすら言えない。どうしよう…。
   I can't talk about this problem even with friends. What should I do...?

4. 日本に行ったことすらない人でも日本人はすごく優しくて礼儀正しいと思っている。
   Even people that have never been to Japan think the people are really friendly and respectful/polite.

5. 辛いのが大好きな彼ですら、この店のカレーは食べられない。
   Even he, who loves spicy food, can't eat this restaurant's curry.

擬音語

Japanese Onomatopoeia – "To look/see/watch"

【きょろきょろ】 Looking around oneself
Ex. 初めて東京に行った時、きょろきょろしながら歩いていた。
The first time I went to Tokyo, I turned my head looking every which way as I was walking.

【じろじろ】 To look at one particular thing intently
Ex. コスプレして町を歩いていたら、みんなからじろじろ見られた。
I dressed up in cosplay and as I walked around town, everyone was staring at me.

【まじまじ】 To look at something one time and then take a closer look
Ex. 彼女は指輪の値段を聞いたとたん、その指輪をまじまじと見た。
As soon as she heard the cost of the ring, she stopped and took a closer look.

単語を並び替えて、文にしなさい。
Unscramble the following words to make sentences.

(1) There is no reaction whatsoever. The experiment seems to have failed.

実験は　さえ　失敗した　反応　何の　ようだ　ない　。

_____ 。

(2) Even after the age of 70, Hokusai never once lost his ambition in his later years.

向上心を　北斎は　失う　晩年　ことはなかった　７０歳を

でさえ　過ぎた

_____ 。

(3) She left town without even saying anything to her family.

肉親　何も　その街を　彼女は　出た　にさえ　言わずに

_____ 。

(4) Even though that kid is 10 years old, he still can't even do addition.

１０歳　足し算　すら　なのに　その子供は　できなかった　もう

_____ 。

(5) The employee couldn't take a day off even for New Year's.

取る　お正月　従業員は　ことは　休みを　できなかった　ですら

_____ 。

(6) This building is designed to withstand even large earthquakes.

なっている　にすら　この建物は　耐えられる　大型地震　構造に

_____ 。

Chapter 72
「〜とすれば / としたら / とすると」&
「〜としても」

I. 「〜とすれば / としたら / とすると」 Assuming that 〜

We can use this grammar structure when we want to make a conjecture or some kind of supposition.
It can be translated as "assuming that..." or "if it is the case that..."

Noun / な-adjective	+ だとすれば / だとしたら / だとすると
Casual-form-verb / い-adjective	+ とすれば / としたら / とすると

1. 彼が言っていることが本当だとしたら、どうすればいいの？
   If what he says is true, what should we do?

2. 彼女が犯人ではないとすれば、誰が私の財布を盗ったんだろう。
   Assuming she is not the criminal, then who was it that stole my wallet?

3. バスで行くとすると、何時間くらいかかりますか？
   If we were to go by bus, how long would it take (how many hours would it take)?

4. ＪＬＰＴ３の文法があなたにとって難しいとしたら、
   もっと簡単な教科書を買えばいい。
   If it is the case that JLPT 3 level grammar is difficult for you, then you should buy
   an easier textbook.

5. この車の方が安全だとしたら、高くても買った方がいいんじゃない？
   Given the case that this car is safer, even if it is more expensive, wouldn't it be better
   to buy it?

6. 太陽がバスケットボールとすると、地球は豆ほどの大きさです。
   If we assume that the sun was a basketball, then the earth would be about the size of a pea.

7. 今日が<u>無理だとしたら</u>、明日はどうですか？

   If today doesn't work, how about tomorrow?

II. 「〜としても」 Even assuming that 〜

This structure is similar to what we learned above, but can be translated as "*even* assuming that..." or "*even* if it is the case that..."

8. たとえ<u>謝ったとしても</u>、許してあげない。

   Even if she were to apologize, I wouldn't forgive her.

9. 彼がどこにいるのか<u>知っていたとしても</u>教えてあげない。

   Even if I did know where he was, I wouldn't tell you.

10. 自分でやるのは<u>無理だとしても</u>、やってみます。

    Even if doing it myself is impossible, I will give it a shot.

11. あの町は<u>不便だとしても</u>、あそこに引っ越したい。

    Even assuming that town is an inconvenient place to live, I still want to move there.

12. 明日は<u>暑いとしても</u>、外でトレーニングをします。

    Even if it is hot tomorrow, I am still going to train outside.

→Answer: P244

「とすれば」、「としたら」、「とすると」、「としても」のいずれかを使って、
2つの文を1つの文にしなさい。

Take the following sentences and combine them into one, using 「とすれば」, 「としたら」,
「とすると」, or 「としても」.

(1) この遺跡は本物。世紀の大発見。

If these remains are real, it will be the discovery of the century!

_____ !

(2) 国のリーダーは愚かです。国民の生活は大変な事になります。

If the leader of a country is foolish, the lives of the citizens will be harsh.

_____ 。

(3) 民宿を営む。どのくらいの資金が必要になるかな。

I wonder how much money you need to run a bed-and-breakfast.

_____ 。

(4) 言い伝えは正しい。このあたりに埋蔵金があるはず。

If the legends are true, there should be buried treasure somewhere in this area.

_____ 。

(5) 彼は20歳です。彼のお母さんは今45歳です。

If he is 20 years old, then that means his mother must be 45.

_____ 。

(6) それが本心です。もっと言葉を選んで伝えるべき。

Even if those are your true feelings, you should choose your words carefully.

_____ 。

Chapter 73
「〜際に / 〜際(に)は」
さい　　　　　　　さい
At the time of 〜/In the event that 〜

This structure is used with both nouns and verbs to express "at the time of" or "in the event that." It has a very similar meaning and usage to「時」, but is much more formal.
とき / じ

Noun
Dictionary-form-verb   } + 際に / 際(に)は
さい　　　　　さい

---

1. 「お降りの際は、お足元にご注意ください。」
   お　　さい　　　　あしもと　　　ちゅうい
   "Please watch your step as you exit."

2. 外出する際は、鍵をかけるのを忘れないでください。
   がいしゅつ　さい　　　かぎ　　　　　　　わす
   When you go out, please be sure to lock the door.

3. 今度長崎へいらっしゃった際には、ぜひ我が家にお泊まりください。
   こんどながさき　　　　　　さい　　　　　　わ　や　　　と
   The next time you come to Nagasaki, please come and stay at my home.

4. 車を運転する際には、運転免許はなくてはならないです。
   くるま　うんてん　さい　　　　うんてんめんきょ
   You must have a driver's license to operate a vehicle.

5. 非常時の際には、この窓ガラスを割って逃げてください。
   ひじょうじ　さい　　　　　　まど　　　　わ　　　に
   In the event of an emergency, please break this window and flee.

6. ビザを申請する際に必要なものは、ここに書いてあります。
   しんせい　さい　ひつよう　　　　　　　　か
   What you need when applying for your visa is written down here.

「際」を使って、文を1つの文にしなさい。

Take the following sentences and combine them into one, using「際」.

(1) 海外旅行をする。パスポートを忘れないでください。

When traveling abroad, please do not forget your passport.

_____ 。

(2) お母さんは掃除をした。メモを捨ててしまった。

Mom threw out that note when she was cleaning.

_____ 。

(3) お会計をする。こちらのカウンターにお越しください。

When paying the bill, please come to this counter.

_____ 。

(4) この万年筆で大事な書類に署名をする。万年筆を使う。

Use this fountain pen when signing important documents.

_____ 。

(5) こちらの資料。お手すき。ご覧ください。

When you have a free moment, please take a look at these materials.

_____ 。

Practice Answers

Chapter 1
(1)　日本語を勉強することは楽しいです。
(2)　毎日ジムに行くことはつらいです。（ジムに毎日行くことはつらいです。）
(3)　一番便利なことはこれ。
(4)　彼女にアメリカに行きたくないことを伝えた。（アメリカに行きたくないことを彼女に伝えた。）
(5)　かわいいことが一番大事。

(6)　てんぷらを食べたことがない。
(7)　日本に行ったことがありますか？
(8)　このゲームをしたことがありますか？
(9)　この本を読んだことがありますか？
(10)　この本を読んだことがない。

(11)　b. したことがない
(12)　d. ことにしている
(13)　a. 言ったこと
(14)　b. ことにしている
(15)　c. ことはないよ
(16)　a. やることは
(17)　b. 住んだこと
(18)　c. ことになっている
(19)　d. 買うことにした
(20)　b. 泣くことは
(21)　a. 買うことにした
(22)　b. ことになっている

Chapter 2
(1)　あれはほしくない。
(2)　彼女はおおきなパソコンはほしくなかった。
(3)　私は黒いのがほしいです。
(4)　これがほしかったら、買ったほうがいい。
(5)　どれがほしいですか？

(6)　私は彼女に犬を買ってほしい。
(7)　私は彼女に行ってほしくない。
(8)　私はお兄ちゃんに家に帰ってきてほしくなかった。
(9)　彼は私に朝ご飯を作ってほしかった。
(10)　私は彼らに勝ってほしかった。
(11)　僕に（これを）書いてほしいの？
(12)　私は両親に来日してほしい。

Chapter 3
(1)　お父さんは何時に帰るか知っていますか？
(2)　何人来るか知っていますか？
(3)　これは誰のか（私は）知りません。
(4)　何が書いてあるか（私は）読めないです。
(5)　彼の誕生日はいつか知っていますか？

Chapter 5
(1) うちの猫が傷だらけになって帰ってきた。
(2) 私は漢字だらけの新聞を読めないです。
(3) 弟の部屋はゴミだらけです。
(4) 彼は歯を磨かないから虫歯だらけです。
(5) 私の宿題は間違いだらけでした。

Chapter 6
(1) 祭りのせいか人が多い。
(2) 寝不足のせいか映画館で寝てしまった。
(3) 建物が古いせいで歩くと床がきしむ。
(4) 彼女は真面目なせいか時々冗談が通じない。
(5) 彼は先生に怒られたせいで、しょんぼりしている。
(6) 寝坊をしたせいで電車に乗り遅れた。

Chapter 7
(1) みたい
(2) くらい/ぐらい
(3) くらい/ぐらい
(4) みたい
(5) くらい/ぐらい
(6) みたい
(7) くらい/ぐらい
(8) みたい

Chapter 8
(1) つもり
(2) つもり
(3) つもり
(4) ことにしている
(5) つもり
(6) ことにしている
(7) ことにしている

Chapter 9
(1) 桜が咲いて春らしくなってきたね。
(2) この本の話は怖いらしい。
(3) 携帯の充電が切れたみたいだ。
(4) 天気予報によると昼から雨になるようだ。
(5) 彼女は毎日豆乳を飲んでいるらしい。（毎日彼女は豆乳を飲んでいるらしい。）
(6) 雨だから今日のキャンプは中止だそうだ。
(7) このアプリは便利らしい。

Chapter 10
(1) 今年の夏は雨が多くなるのではないかと思う。
(2) あのスタッフは、真理さんの妹なのではないだろうか。
(3) 宝くじをずっと買い続けていれば、いつかは当たるだろう。
(4) この椅子は子供にとっては高いのではないだろうか。
(5) この機能は邪魔なのではないかと思う。
(6) 彼は一生結婚しないつもりだろうか。
(7) 今日の飲み会は何時からだろうか？

Chapter 11
(1)　　c.　ておかないと
(2)　　a.　ておいて
(3)　　d.　でおきましたか
(4)　　b.　でおこう
(5)　　a.　ておいて
(6)　　d.　ておけば
(7)　　b.　ておきましたか
(8)　　c.　ておこうか

Chapter 12
(1)　　この変な服を着るくらいなら、裸のほうがいい。
(2)　　後悔するくらいなら、やったほうがいい。
(3)　　（列に）並ぶくらいなら、ジェットコースターに乗らない。
(4)　　満員電車に乗るくらいなら、タクシーに乗る。
(5)　　梅干を食べるくらいなら、納豆を食べる方がましだ。

Chapter 13
(1)　　この音色は琴に違いない。
(2)　　彼女は書道を習い始めたに違いない。
(3)　　新幹線は速いに違いない。
(4)　　このアルバイトは楽に違いない。
(5)　　今、吠えたのは、あの犬に違いない。
(6)　　歌舞伎を観ても、なんて言っているか分からないに違いない。
(7)　　案内係りのスタッフは親切に違いない。

Chapter 14
(1)　　おにぎりは美味しいに決まってる。
(2)　　このメーカーの製品は長持ちするに決まっている。
(3)　　グランドキャニオンは壮大に決まっている。
(4)　　今の季節、外は肌寒いに決まっている。
(5)　　この計画は無茶に決まっている。

Chapter 15
(1)　　a.　閲覧するようになっている
(2)　　c.　ように
(3)　　d.　ような
(4)　　c.　ようがない
(5)　　b.　遅刻しないように
(6)　　c.　できないようになっている
(7)　　d.　ないように
(8)　　b.　ような

Chapter 16
(1)　　b.　わけがある
(2)　　a.　わけなく
(3)　　b.　なわけだ
(4)　　d.　しないわけにはいかない
(5)　　c.　わけがない
(6)　　b.　わけが分からない
(7)　　a.　わけだ
(8)　　d.　わけではない

Chapter 17

(1) 弁護士だからといって、全ての法律を知っているとは限らない。
(2) おしゃれだからといって、たくさん服を持っているとは限らない。
(3) 仲がいいからといって、ずっと一緒にいるとは限らない。
(4) お酒が好きだからといって、たくさん飲めるとは限らない。
(5) 照れくさいからといって、彼女に冷たくしない方がいい。
(6) 体調が良くなったからといって、調子に乗ってはだめですよ。
(7) 高価なバックだからといって、使わないのはもったいないよ。

Chapter 18

(1) お腹が減ってたまらない。
(2) ひとり暮らしはさみしくてたまらない。
(3) ペットの猫が愛しくてたまらない。
(4) 心細くてたまらなかったけど、だんだん慣れてきた。
(5) この本の初めはばかばかしくてたまらなかったけど、徐々に面白くなってきた。

Chapter 19

(1) 授業は 10 時から 12 時にかけて行われた。
(2) 渋滞は住宅地から駅前にかけて続いている。
(3) 車で名古屋から東京にかけて行った。/車で名古屋から東京にかけて運転した。

Chapter 20

(1) 日本語を勉強したおかげで、漫画を読めるようになった。
(2) みなさんのおかげで、留学生活は楽しかったです。
(3) 仕事が楽なせいで、どんどん怠け者になってきた。
(4) 目覚まし時計のおかげで、ちゃんと起きられた。
(5) 旅館のサービスがきめ細かいおかげで、とてもリラックスできた。

Chapter 21

(1) 鍵を閉めたっけ？
(2) 猫に朝ご飯をあげたっけ？
(3) 彼が来たのは昨日だったっけ？
(4) この話の最後はこんなにつまらなかったっけ？
(5) ここの入場料は（大人も小人も）一律だっけ？

Chapter 22

(1) ちゃ
(2) じゃう
(3) じゃ
(4) ちゃう
(5) ちゃった
(6) ちゃ
(7) じゃった
(8) じゃ

Chapter 23

(1) このことに関しては、私は何も知りません。
(2) 彼女のペンギンに関する知識は、とても豊富だ。
(3) この会議で(は)、環境保護について話し合われます。
(4) 彼は将来に関して悲観的だ。
(5) 昨日、（私は）お父さんに仕事に関する相談をした。
(6) 山本さんは文学について無関心だ。

Chapter 24
(1)　今年は去年に比べて雨が多い。
(2)　彼の成績は以前に比べてかなり良くなった。
(3)　茶道に比べて香道はあまり知られていない。
(4)　九州弁に比べて大阪弁は早口だ。
(5)　この製品は従来に比べてかなり軽くなった。

Chapter 25
(1)　夜が更けるにつれて月が輝いてきた。
(2)　音楽に従って踊りましょう。
(3)　科学の進歩につれて生活の知恵が失われていった。
(4)　本棚をマニュアルに従い組み立てた。
(5)　月日が経つに従って悲しみは大きくなってきた。
(6)　台風が近づくに従い風が強くなってきた。

Chapter 26
(1)　日本に住んでいたにしては、日本のことをあまり知らないね。
(2)　彼女は控えめなわりには、とても強い意志を持っている。
(3)　ソファにしては軽いね。一人で動かせるよ。
(4)　渡辺さんは用心深いわりに、すぐ物をなくす。
(5)　値段のわりには、いい製品だと思う。
(6)　私はよく食べるわりには、太りません。

Chapter 27
(1)　中村さんは若いのにしっかりしている。
(2)　このトレッキングコースは過酷なのに人気がある。
(3)　一生懸命に踊ったのに、みんなから笑われた。
(4)　この本が書かれたのは千年前なのに、とても近代的な内容だ。
(5)　銀閣寺に銀は使われていないのに、銀閣寺と呼ばれている。
(6)　私は真剣なのに、彼は真面目に話を聞いてくれない。

Chapter 28
(1)　やるなら今しかない！
(2)　私は今 100 円しか持っていない。
(3)　これができるのは、あなたしかいない。
(4)　この指輪には少しの価値しかない。
(5)　誕生日は 1 年に 1 回しかない。
(6)　私はイタリアにしか行ったことがない。

Chapter 29
(1)　犯人は黒っぽい服を着ていたらしい。
(2)　このコーヒーは水っぽくて美味しくない。
(3)　あの女優さんはとても色っぽいね。
(4)　小林さんは短気で怒りっぽい。
(5)　彼は飽きっぽいからどんなことも長続きしない。

Chapter 30
(1)　買い物に行くたびに服を買ってしまう。
(2)　彼を見るたびに胸がときめく。
(3)　皿洗いのたびに彼は皿を割る。（彼は皿洗いのたびに皿を割る。）
(4)　環境の変化のたびに生き物は進化した。（生き物は環境の変化のたびに進化した。）
(5)　会うたびに加藤さんは若くなっていく。（加藤さんは会うたびに若くなっていく。）

Chapter 31

(1) とたん（に）
(2) とたん（に）
(3) につれて
(4) とたん（に）
(5) につれて

Chapter 32

(1) 3年のうちに100万円を貯めようと思う。
(2) 温かいうちに召し上がってください。
(3) 渋滞しないうちに帰宅します。
(4) お母さんが穏やかなうちに部屋を片付けた方がいい。
(5) 生きているうちに一度は南極に行ってみたい。
(6) お父さんが帰ってくるのを待っているうちに寝てしまった。
(7) この研究は秘密のうちに進められていた。

Chapter 33

(1) 彼女が清楚なものか！男勝りの性格だよ。
(2) 福岡が田舎なものか。日本で3番目の都市だよ。
(3) 足を怪我しているのだから、軽快に歩けるものか。
(4) 最近の長崎はのどかなものか。お祭りでとても賑やかだよ。
(5) 子猫が鬱陶しいものか。可愛くて仕方がないよ。
(6) きみの意見に反対なものか。大賛成だよ！
(7) そんなふざけたことを厳しい山田さんに言えるものか。

Chapter 34

(1) 彼女は消極的なものだから（もので）、なかなか場になじめない。
(2) 不思議なもので、お守りを持っていると勇気がわいてくる。
(3) 彼女の嫌悪感は露骨なもので（なものだから）、誰もが彼女に気を遣っていた。
(4) 別れが名残惜しいものだから（もので）、私達は何度も抱き合った。
(5) 子供が生まれたものだから、毎日早く帰りたいのだ。
(6) すみません、急いでいるもので（ものだから）、そろそろ失礼します。
(7) これは規則なものだから、仕方がない。
(8) 朝はすがすがしいもので、深呼吸するとより気持ちがいい。

Chapter 35

(1) 今晩は、豪雨になる恐れがある（豪雨の恐れがある）。
(2) このままだと、会社をクビになる恐れがある。
(3) 雪が降っているので、路面凍結の恐れがある。
(4) その言い方だと、誤解される恐れがある。
(5) しっかりと治療をしないと、再発の恐れがある（再発する恐れがある）。
(6) 近いうちに株価暴落の恐れがある。

Chapter 36

(1) 電話に出ないということは、山口さんは今忙しいということだね。
(2) 指輪をもらったということは、彼女はプロポーズされたということだね。
(3) 彼が詐欺師だったということは、私は騙されたということだ。
(4) ここにあったクッキーがないということは、誰かが食べてしまったということだね。
(5) 平成3年生まれということは、私と同級生ということだね。

(6) きっと全て上手くいくから、何も気にすることはないよ。
(7) 希望がないこともないが、あまり期待しない方がいいだろう。
(8) 毎日が目まぐるしいことはないが、そこそこ忙しい。

(9) iPad を持っていないことはないが、使い方が分からない。

(10) その計画は途方もないこともないが、人手が足りないと思う。

Chapter 37

(1) たとえ和食でも、食べ過ぎたら太ってしまう。

(2) 子供達がたとえ生意気でも、決して怒鳴ってはいけないよ。

(3) たとえ短い時間でも、彼女に会いたかった。

(4) たとえばかばかしくても、これはやらなければいけない。

(5) たとえ笑われても、私はこの髪型が好きだから気にしない。

(6) 講義がたとえ退屈でも、最後まで受けなければいけない。

(7) その俳優がたとえ日本で有名でも、世界で有名とは限らない。

Chapter 38

(1) これは自然にとって優しい商品です。

(2) いつがあなたにとって都合がいいですか？（あなたにとっていつが都合がいいですか？）

(3) 私にとって、父の姉は伯母になります。

(4) 花火が好きな人にとっては、花火大会は待ち遠しいイベントです。

(5) 私にとって留学することは勇気がいることでした。

Chapter 39

(1) やると決めたからには最善を尽くす。

(2) ここまで来たからには後戻りできない。

(3) こんなことするからには何か考えがあるのだよね？

(4) 成人になったからには自分の行動に責任を持ちなさい。

(5) 奨学金をもらったからには一生懸命勉強しなければいけない。

Chapter 40

(1) b. 置いたはず

(2) c. するはずがない

(3) a. です

(4) d. 望ましいはず

(5) c. 必死なはずだ

(6) a. 派手なはず

(7) d. 肌寒いはずだ

Chapter 41

(1) あんな危険なことは二度とやるな（やらないで）！

(2) ずる休みをするな（しないで）！

(3) お菓子ばかり食べるな（食べないで）！

(4) 私の話を無視しないで（するな）！

Chapter42

(1) 林さんの家に行ったら、お昼ご飯の最中だった。

(2) 現在、原因を調査している最中です。

(3) お話の最中にすみません。

(4) 台風の最中に外に出てはいけません。

(5) 今、ビザの申請をしている最中です。

Chapter 43

(1) b. 800 円だって

(2) b. 圧倒的だって

(3) a. 回りくどいって

(4) c. 休むって

(5)　d.　あっけないらしい
(6)　b.　臆病だって
(7)　d.　分かったって
(8)　a.　梅です

Chapter 44
(1)　a.　南向き
(2)　b.　入学者向け
(3)　c.　左を向いている
(4)　a.　前向き
(5)　c.　上向き
(6)　d.　あっち向き
(7)　d.　どっち向き

Chapter 45
(1)　今、テレビを観ているから、話しかけないで。
(2)　危なかった！彼に騙されかけた！
(3)　読みかけの小説だから、しおりを動かさないでね。
(4)　途中で投げ出しかけたが、頑張って最後までやり遂げた。
(5)　彼女は何かを言いかけたが、何も言わずに去って行った。
(6)　やりかけの仕事があるから、また職場に戻らなきゃ。
(7)　彼女の見せかけの優しさに惑わされた。

Chapter 46
(1)　今日はしんどくてならない。
(2)　何か悪いことが起こる気がしてならない。
(3)　彼の死は無念でならない。
(4)　僕の猫をいじめたあの犬が憎たらしくてたまらない。
(5)　温泉は心地よくてたまらない。（温泉は心地よくてたまらん。）
(6)　私は、これは偶然ではないと思えてならない。
(7)　彼女の行動は愚かでならない。

Chapter 47
(1)　花は愛情を注げば注ぐほど綺麗に咲く。（愛情を注げば注ぐほど、花は綺麗に咲く。）
(2)　経験は強烈ならば強烈なほど記憶に残る。
(3)　野菜はみずみずしければ、みずみずしいほど新鮮だと言うことです。
(4)　授業をさぼればさぼるほど卒業できなくなるよ。
(5)　マジックのテクニックが巧妙ならば巧妙なほど面白い。

Chapter 48
(1)　お正月以来、お餅を食べていない。
(2)　彼と別れて以来、誰とも付き合っていない。
(3)　卒業以来、恩師とは会っていません。
(4)　日本に行くのは、去年の出張以来です。
(5)　妊娠して以来、ずっと禁酒している。
(6)　その事件が発生して以来、テレビでは毎日そのニュースが流れている。

Chapter 49
(1)　その国は軍事力に対し、経済力が弱い。
(2)　この薬は、風邪に対して効かない。
(3)　アリゾナに対して、興味が湧いてきた。
(4)　彼に対して少し言い過ぎた。
(5)　彼の無礼な態度に対し、彼女はとても上品に対応した。

(6)　政治家の権力に対し、市民は団結力で抗議した。

Chapter 50
(1)　情熱を込めてピアノを弾く。
(2)　悲しみを込めて、その台詞を言う。
(3)　真心を込めて、料理を作った。
(4)　渾身の力を込めて、サンドバックを殴った。
(5)　戒めの意を込めて、落ちた試験の結果を壁に貼った。

Chapter 51
(1)　この国の景気は悪くなる一方だ。
(2)　漫画が大好きだから、漫画本が増える一方だ。
(3)　彼は謝る一方で、理由は教えてくれなかった。
(4)　地球温暖化で、気温は高くなる一方だ。
(5)　その定員のせいで、彼の怒りは募る一方だった。
(6)　彼の会社の業績は傾く一方だ。

Chapter 52
(1)　私の記憶によると、小さい頃この川に来たことがあります。
(2)　子供達の話によれば、この森にはリスがいるらしい。
(3)　聞くところによると、彼は生真面目な性格らしいです。
(4)　研究結果によると、にんにくは癌を予防するそうです。
(5)　伝説によれば、この泉の水を飲むと長生きするらしい。
(6)　AI の計算によれば、地球の平均気温はさらに上がるらしい。

Chapter 53
(1)　私は今起床したところです。（今、私は起床したところです。）
(2)　子供達が寝る頃に、お父さんが帰ってきた。
(3)　横断歩道を渡ろうとしたところ、猛スピードで車が走ってきた。（車が猛スピードで走ってきた。）
(4)　彼のことを考えていたところ、彼から電話がかかってきた。
(5)　叔父の家を訪ねたところ、留守だった。

Chapter 54
(1)　手を洗ってからでないと、おやつを食べてはいけない。
(2)　地盤を調査してからでなければ、ビルは建てられない。
(3)　データを保存してからでないと、パソコンを閉じてはいけない。
(4)　しっかり点検してからでなければ、その車には乗ってはいけない。
(5)　アンケートに答えてからでないと、あれはもらえないよ。

Chapter 55
(1)　私は本音のかわりに建前を言うことがあります。
(2)　鍋で温めるかわりに電子レンジで温めた。
(3)　経済成長が著しいかわりに、衰退も早い。
(4)　彼は生真面目なかわりに融通が利かない。
(5)　私は肉にかわり、大豆でタンパク質を摂取している。
(6)　昨今は年賀状にかわって、メールで新年の挨拶をする人が増えてきた。

Chapter 56
(1)　だけ
(2)　だけ
(3)　だけ
(4)　なだけ

Chapter 57

(1)　b. たばかり
(2)　a. ばかり
(3)　c. するばかり
(4)　b. たばかり
(5)　c. ばかりに
(6)　d. あるばかりに
(7)　d. ばかりに
(8)　c. とばかりに

(9)　弟ばかりでなく僕もお母さんに怒られた。
(10)　「日」と「曰」は紛らわしいばかりではなく、画数も同じだ。
(11)　彼は言うばかりでなく行動もする。
(12)　阿部さんは話が上手なばかりではなく、聞き上手でもある。
(13)　永野さんはその難しい方程式を理解するばかりか応用することもできる。
(14)　なにより彼は浮気ばかりか借金もする最低の夫だった。
(15)　そのおばあさんは朗らかなばかりか、上品な人でもあった。

Chapter 58

(1)　この費用も見積もりに加えてください。
(2)　新しい社員を加え、弊社はより一層サービスを拡充しました。
(3)　中村さんはいつもビールとともに枝豆を食べる。
(4)　高齢化とともに人口減少も深刻な問題になりつつある。
(5)　技術者は、ノートパソコンの軽量化を図るとともに省電力化にも注力している。

Chapter 59

(1)　一個人としては、彼女の見解に賛同する。
(2)　事実として、魚の消費量が世界的に増えてきている。
(3)　これまで義務教育を当然のこととして受けてきた。（義務教育をこれまで当然のこととして受けてきた。）
(4)　あの話はなかったこととして考えてください。
(5)　秀才でも時として間違えることもある。

Chapter 60

(1)　ジェレミーは、日本語はもとより英語もスペイン語も話せる。
(2)　母親はとっさに子供はもちろんペットの犬もかばった。
(3)　異常な暑さだから、もちろんクーラーをつけているよ。
(4)　このメーカーの商品は、機能性はもちろん安全性も高い。
(5)　案の定、彼は飛行機のチケットはもとよりパスポートも忘れてきた。

Chapter 61

(1)　若者の迅速な行動をきっかけに、ボランティアの輪が広がった。
(2)　あの事件をきっかけにして、新しい法律が制定された。
(3)　妻の妊娠をきっかけとして、僕はタバコをやめました。
(4)　周辺地域の騒音がきっかけで、私は引っ越すことにした。
(5)　ハワイに行ったことがきっかけで、ハワイの音楽が好きになった。

Chapter 62

(1)　リスクは分散するべきです。
(2)　不満があっても暴力に訴えるべきではない。
(3)　怒って帰る彼女を追うべきか追わざるべきか彼は悩んだ。
(4)　この先注意すべし。
(5)　授業を無断で欠席するべきではないよ。

Chapter 63
(1) 地震の発生にともない、広い地域で停電が起こった。
(2) オリンピックの開催にともなって、街のインフラが整ってきた。
(3) 日が沈むにともない、だんだん赤焼け空になってきた。
(4) 台風の勢力が強まるにともなって、風も強くなってきた。
(5) 出産のときの陣痛はかなりの痛みを伴います。

Chapter 64
(1) 彼は厳しい上司である半面、頼れる指導者でもある。
(2) ペンギンは飛行能力が退化した半面、泳ぐ能力が備わった。
(3) 生意気な子供は憎たらしい半面、愛おしくもある。
(4) トライアスロンは過酷な半面、ゴールした時の達成感が大きい。

Chapter 65
(1) コーヒーを淹れるついでにいつも甘いものをつまんでしまう。
(2) 子猿を保護したついでに、怪我の手当をしてあげた。
(3) 話のついでに、離婚の手続きについて相談してみた。
(4) 引っ越すついでに、家具を全て新調することにした。
(5) 出張で福岡に行ったついでに、おばさんに会いに行った。

Chapter 66
(1) 漁師のくせに、魚料理が嫌いだなんて変なの。
(2) 何も知らないくせに、知ったような口を利かないで！
(3) 本当は心細いくせに、強がっちゃって。
(4) 男のくせに人前で泣くなんて、情けないね。
(5) その子供は臆病なくせに、お化け屋敷に入りたがる。
(6) 疲れているくせに、どうして友達からの誘いを断らないの？

Chapter 67
(1) b. やりっぱなし
(2) a. 鳴りっぱなし
(3) c. 開けっぱなし（あけっぱなし）
(4) d. 打ちっぱなし
(5) c. のろけっぱなし

Chapter 68
(1) b. きれない
(2) c. しきった
(3) a. きって
(4) d. きれなさそうな
(5) a. 見きれない

Chapter 69
(1) 吉田さんは親に頼らずに自分で大学の学費を払った。
(2) その棋士は、子供相手でも手加減せずに将棋を指した。
(3) 彼の間抜けな失敗に呆れずにはいられない。
(4) 彼女はためらわずにバンジージャンプを飛んだ。
(5) あの人の生い立ちには同情せずにはいられない。

Chapter 70
(1) この壁はペンキ塗りたてだから、気をつけてね。
(2) 日本に来たての人にとっては、このガイドブックはとても役に立つと思う。
(3) ファーマーズマーケットでは、採れたて野菜が買える。

(4) おじさんの農園を手伝うと、もぎたてのリンゴが食べられる。
(5) 結婚したての頃は、料理があまり上手ではありませんでした。

Chapter 71
(1) お金さえあれば、今すぐハワイに行くのに。
(2) 生きてさえいれば、いつかは会えるよ。
(3) 人工知能（AI）は学習することさえできるらしい。
(4) 夢の中でさえも日本語を勉強していた。
(5) この問題は私にさえ分かるような簡単なものだ。

(6) 何の反応さえない。実験は失敗したようだ。
(7) 北斎は70歳を過ぎた晩年でさえ向上心を失うことはなかった。
(8) 彼女は肉親にさえ何も言わずにその街を出た。
(9) その子供はもう10歳なのに足し算すらできなかった。
(10) 従業員はお正月ですら休みを取ることはできなかった。
(11) この建物は大型地震にすら耐えられる構造になっている。

Chapter 72
(1) この遺跡が本物だとすれば、世紀の大発見だ！
(2) 国のリーダーが愚かだとしたら、国民の生活は大変なことになります。
(3) 民宿を営むとしたら、どのくらいの資金が必要になるかな。
(4) 言い伝えが正しいとすれば、この辺りに埋蔵金があるはず。
(5) 彼が20歳だとすると、彼のお母さんは今45歳です。
(6) それが本心だとしても、もっと言葉を選んで伝えるべきです。

Chapter 73
(1) 海外旅行する際には、パスポートを忘れないでください。
(2) お母さんは掃除の際にそのメモを捨ててしまった。
(3) お会計の際には、こちらのカウンターにお越しください。
(4) この万年筆は、大事な書類に署名をする際に使います。
(5) こちらの資料は、お手すきの際にご覧ください。

ありがとうございます!

If you have made it to the end of this book, おめでとうございます! I hope that you found it helpful and that your Japanese improved as a result.

Remember, learning Japanese (or any language) takes a lot of time and effort. You will need to review the chapters in this book multiple times before you can fully take in the content. Don't be discouraged if you found something difficult to grasp the first time you took a crack at it. My advice, in those situations, is to just move on and go back to what was giving you difficulty at a later date. In my experience, you will find that what you thought was difficult to understand will suddenly click and make perfect sense.

I also want to thank everyone who helped me and encouraged me to start and finish this book: The biggest thanks goes to 美緑, who edited and designed the interior of this book and without whom I would have never finished, my mom and dad for always motivating me and supporting me in whatever I do, and my friends for making my time spent in Japan so amazing and helping me learn.

Thanks again, dear reader, I hope I could help you in some way in achieving your Japanese related dreams,

Jeremy

Find me on YouTube at: https://www.youtube.com/LearnJapaneseFromSomeGuy

Check out my homepage: www.LearnJapaneseFromSomeGuy.com

My first beginner level textbook Learn Japanese From Some Guy can be found on Amazon here: https://www.amazon.com/dp/B013D2FDMG

If you are interested in teaching English abroad, you can find my book titled Teach English Abroad on Amazon at: https://www.amazon.com/dp/B01N41JZ8R

Ingram Content Group UK Ltd.
Milton Keynes UK
UKHW050713260723
425809UK00014B/482